Another Way Home

Another Way Home

The Tangled Roots of Race in One Chicago Family

RONNE HARTFIELD

THE UNIVERSITY OF CHICAGO PRESS · *Chicago & London*

RONNE HARTFIELD *is a senior research fellow in religion and art at the Harvard University Center for the Study of World Religions and an international museum consultant. She is the former Woman's Board Endowed Executive Director of Museum Education at the Art Institute of Chicago and former executive director of Chicago-based Urban Gateways: The Center for Arts in Education.*

The University of Chicago Press, Chicago 60637
The University of Chicago Press, Ltd., London
© 2004 by Ronne Hartfield
All rights reserved. Published 2004
Printed in the United States of America

13 12 11 10 09 08 07 06 05 04   1 2 3 4 5

ISBN: 0-226-31821-4 (cloth)

Library of Congress Cataloging-in-Publication Data

Hartfield, Ronne, 1936–
     Another way home : the tangled roots of race in one Chicago family /
     Ronne Hartfield.
         p.   cm.
      ISBN 0-226-31821-4 (cloth : alk. paper)
      1. Hartfield, Ronne, 1936–. 2. Racially mixed people—Illinois—
Chicago—Biography. 3. Chicago (Ill.)—Biography. 4. United States—
Race relations—Case studies. I. Title.

F548.25.H37   2004
977.3′110040596073′0092—dc22
[B]

                                                          2003027030

For our clan

CONTENTS

Photographs follow page 76

Family Tree

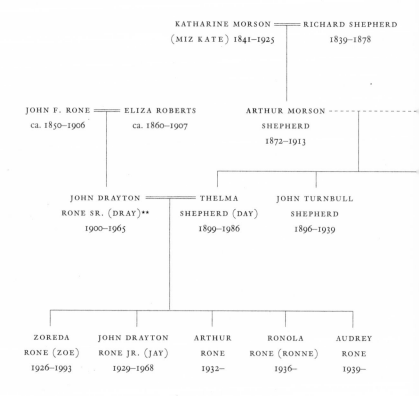

KATHARINE MORSON ═══ RICHARD SHEPHERD
(MIZ KATE) 1841–1925   1839–1878

JOHN F. RONE ═══ ELIZA ROBERTS   ARTHUR MORSON - - - - - - - - - - -
ca. 1850–1906   ca. 1860–1907   SHEPHERD
                                     1872–1913

JOHN DRAYTON ═══ THELMA   JOHN TURNBULL
RONE SR. (DRAY)**   SHEPHERD (DAY)   SHEPHERD
1900–1965   1899–1986   1896–1939

ZOREDA   JOHN DRAYTON   ARTHUR   RONOLA   AUDREY
RONE (ZOE)   RONE JR. (JAY)   RONE   RONE (RONNE)   RONE
1926–1993   1929–1968   1932–   1936–   1939–

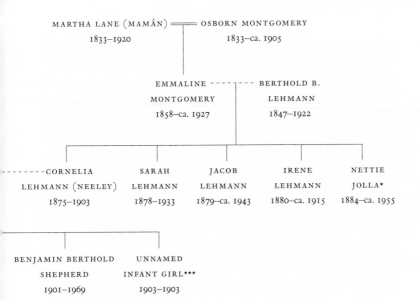

MARTHA LANE (MAMÁN) ══════ OSBORN MONTGOMERY
1833–1920   1833–ca. 1905

EMMALINE - - - - ┐- - - BERTHOLD B.
MONTGOMERY   LEHMANN
1858–ca. 1927   1847–1922

- - - - - - - -CORNELIA   SARAH   JACOB   IRENE   NETTIE
LEHMANN (NEELEY)   LEHMANN   LEHMANN   LEHMANN   JOLLA*
1875–1903   1878–1933   1879–ca. 1943   1880–ca. 1915   1884–ca. 1955

BENJAMIN BERTHOLD   UNNAMED
SHEPHERD   INFANT GIRL***
1901–1969   1903–1903

Marriage	═══════════════════════
Marriage Forbidden	- -
Children / Siblings	───────────────────────

* Berthold B. Lehmann was not the father of Nettie Jolla. Family legend has it that her father was Solomon Jolla. ** John Drayton Rone Sr. was the youngest of fourteen children. *** Cornelia Lehmann lost two other infants at birth.

My mother, Thelma Shepherd Rone, also known as Dearest, or Day.
Wedding portrait, June 1924. With her hair marcel-waved in a fashionable
1920s bob, Day wore this dark brown silk dress for the secret wedding.
A white dress could have raised questions.

PROLOGUE

You have to know your history. Then you'll have a
purposeful presence in the world.

· AUGUST WILSON

The average struggling non-morbid Negro is the best-kept
secret in America.

· ZORA NEALE HURSTON

This memory tale of my mother's life begins with
rivers. We come from river people, from Africa and England and
Germany, whose lives came together unanticipatedly on the
banks of a great river. My mother was raised walking distance
from the Mississippi River, and her view of the world was indelibly shaped by the agricultural riches of that valley, by the
prospering merchant culture that thrived on its travel routes,
and by the accepted mandate of hard work that was the foundation of its social as well as economic life.

My mother's father, Arthur Shepherd, was a wealthy white
plantation owner whose forebears on the Shepherd side included
Virginia military heroes, newly emigrated from England, who
fought against the land of their beginnings in the Revolutionary
War, and Southern patriots who fought Indians and were said to

have been killed by the feared Murrell River pirates. Shepherds founded an eponymous town in what is now West Virginia, nearly contiguous to Antietam, one of the bloodiest of Civil War battle sites. Ironically, Shepherdstown is also adjacent to Harpers Ferry, where John Brown, infamous in Shepherd epistolary history, staged one of the most valiant rebellions on behalf of the slaves ever recorded, and the town founded by my slave-owning ancestors is only a few miles away from Charles Town, the site of John Brown's imprisonment and hanging. The Shepherds built prospering plantations near the Mississippi River, on both the Louisiana and the Mississippi sides. Their wealth burgeoned during and after slavery until finally the boll weevil infiltration at the outset of World War I and the increasing emigration of the black labor force to the north brought an end to that era, and my mother's life took another path.

The Shepherd stream had been mingled with another immigrant tributary, this one bearing the history of affluent German Jewish merchants, the Lehmanns, who settled near Natchez just at the end of the Civil War. They, too, prospered in the busy trade along the river road, founding stores that sold or bartered everything people needed. It was here that one of them, Berthold, spoken of in the Deep South vernacular as "Berthaw," met my maternal great-grandmother, a colored seamstress who bought fabrics in the store, fell in love with her, and fathered several of her children.

This formidable matriarch was herself the product of an illicit liaison between a white slaveowner and an African slave, and it is this lineage that introduces the third tributary of my ancestral stream. The particular names and histories of our slave progenitors are lost to us, but we know this much: that they were among the unnamed legion of Africans transported to the American South to plant and harvest cotton and corn, sorghum and sugarcane, on the endless fecund acres of bottomland that were the foundations of that region's prosperity. We know that, enslaved, they learned how to find their way in this strange new place by following the river.

The music and poetry of black America sings with the power of rivers, and poignant lyrics tell of crossing the river to a spiritual freedom that was far deeper than simply safety on the land. To cross the river sometimes meant, as the song says, to cross over to a *spiritual*, not literal, campground.

A proverb told to Yoruba children teaches that if a river forgets its source, it dries up. Because the world we inhabit now is like a river at floodtide, rushing ahead so rapidly that the ways of one generation are swept away and lost to the next, it seems increasingly important to document what we know to be our *source*. Much of what I know of my own source first came down to me through my mother's gift of storytelling.

This book contains a century of stories that have implications both for history and for how we live now. These are mostly my mother's stories as she told them to me and to my sisters and brothers, in a narrative that didn't really think of itself that way. Her name was Day Shepherd. Officially Thelma Shepherd, she was always called Dearest; in the soft, slow cadence of her Southern homeland, the sound of her name was Day-rest or, nearly always, just Day.

Our mother's roots are entangled in several generations of intricate racial hybridity. In the past two centuries, particularly, mixed-race people like her were called *mulattoes*, a term with dismaying etymological origins in another kind of hybrid, the mule. From this distinctly nonthoroughbred animal, produced by the mating of a donkey and a mare, we move to the "tragic mulatto" stereotype, that wretched creature, familiar to us in literature and film, who cannot find a place of ease on either side of the color line. One of the most enduring classics of that genre is James Weldon Johnson's 1912 *Autobiography of an Ex-Colored Man*. This sad tale of the agonies of those torn between two worlds established a certain place in the pantheon for its author. Ironically though, it was an earlier and very different work that earned literary immortality for Johnson and his brother Rosamond. Their anthem of profound spiritual strength, *Lift Every Voice and Sing*, written in 1900 for a celebration of Abraham Lincoln's birthday, is now enshrined as the Black National Anthem. The shift from its earlier title, *Negro* National Anthem, reflects changes in the vocabularies common at particular times. My own use of race terms throughout this volume also reflects prevalent nomenclatures. Thus the earlier term *colored* transmutes first into *Negro*, then later into *black*, and still later into *African American*, although many members of our family never did give up use of the term *colored*—which is why I employ the latter term throughout much of this book.

Mulattoness, however, has never ceased to be a problem in the literatures of people of color. *Passing* and *Quicksand*, widely read novels by Nella Larsen, a contemporary of the Johnsons, also dramatize the fate of tragic mulattoes. Protagonists are portrayed as torn between two races, their psyches afflicted by confusion and neurosis, their lives ending in profound and permanent shame or even suicide.

As we enter a new century, new tales often confirm these still prevalent stereotypes of tragic mulattoes. Present-day novels and biographies continue to reference the emotional and cultural dislocation of those people who occupy a special zone between the races. Very recent examples include Rebecca Walker's *Half-Black, Half-Jewish*; Neil Henry's *Pearl's Secret: A Black Man's Search for His White Family*; and a wide-ranging anthology of essays titled *Half and Half: Writers on Growing Up Biracial and Bicultural*, edited and introduced by Claudine Chiawei O'Hearn. One of the most bitter and disturbing in this latter collection is Danzy Senna's essay *The Mulatto Millennium*, with its intriguing lexicon of *Variations on a Theme of a Mulatto*, including "Fauxlatto," and "Blulatto," the latter being "a highly rare breed of 'blue-blood' mulatto who can trace their lineage back to the Mayflower."

Some of these stories, those of what Senna might call the "Nouveaulatto" sort, are quite dramatic, and they often include climactic moments of identity formulation. In any bookstore one can find fictional and nonfictional forays into the troubled and conflicted lives of people of mixed race and, increasingly, documentation of searches for long-lost white antecedents, discoveries of shadowy mysteries, hints and family rumors that wouldn't go away. Siblings are sometimes divided, like Johnson's and Larsen's protagonists, as some hide their true backgrounds and pass over into the white world while others, like my mother, choose firmly to live as colored. Although less well known, there are examples of that choice in the literature as well. At the turn of the century, authors like Francis Watkins and Pauline Hopkins wrote of the strengths and loyalties of those of mixed race who might well have forsaken their heritage of color, but instead made the decision for racial solidarity.

What strikes me is the dearth of stories about the ordinary lives of the vast number of people of color who have occupied the zone of mixed race with ease and sanity for several generations, ordinary nontragic people who, within the category of mulattoness, are productive citizens whose lives, individually and within their communities, are emotionally healthy and socially instructive. The special predicament of being born and reared in a family where open miscegenation was the rule and not the exception certainly was formative in shaping my mother's character, but it became for her a resource for strength, creativity, and courage.

As Zora Neale Hurston has noted, the literatures and lives of ordinary black people are mostly well-kept secrets. Narratives of emotional and social health in black families continue to be less available than stories supporting the idea that simply to *be* black in America is to be pathological. Certainly the most widely circulated books written by and about black life fall into this latter category: Richard Wright's *Native Son* and *Black Boy;* Ralph Ellison's *Invisible Man;* James Baldwin's *Go Tell It On the Mountain;* and, more recently, Toni Morrison's *Beloved* and *The Bluest Eye* and Alice Walker's *The Color Purple.* While we celebrate the literary merit, often genius, of these now classic works, the imbalance within the pantheon is notable. Save the more salutary though no less complex tales presented so affectingly in Lorraine Hansberry's *Raisin in the Sun* and Ernest Gaines's *The Autobiog-*

raphy of Miss Jane Pittman, students of African-American literature, both black and white, may well develop a distorted sense
of lived black realities.

Social and psychological dislocation in the canon of black literature has an undeniable foundation in actuality, as the historical predicament of people of color in the United States is indeed
fraught with the calamitous legacy of slavery and continuing
racial oppression. When any person of color encounters these
tragic tales, there is some resonance deep within our cultural inheritance. Readers should and do connect in a real and visceral
way with the histories recounted, which function almost as
scriptural records. However, one wishes still for another layer of
connection and resonance. Tenderness and humor, family unity
and affection, the ordinary dailiness of work and discipline and
order have always provided a backdrop and a maturing context
for many of our lives. Those are as present and as meaningful
and as characteristic of black life as the tragedies that occupy
the largest places in our literatures.

Stories that balance the sorrowful truths of black life with the
simple pleasures of growing up in a healthy black community,
while arguably less dramatic and less prevalent, may be more
common than one might assume. In Ossie Davis's wonderful
play *Purlie Victorious* one of the characters says, "It's a whole lot
of fun being colored—when ain't nobody looking." This line inevitably gets a burst of collusive laughter from black audiences.
I have wanted to write about my family because we really *did*
have a whole lot of fun being colored, and I want my readers to
look at and celebrate that truth. I hope my book will make visible how one colored family created meaningful lives. We are a
family that is, like most families, at once ordinary and extraordinary, typical in some regards, unique in others. These stories
recount the quotidian detail of how we ate and worked and
played and grieved, and of how one family's inner conviction,
resilience, and inventiveness functioned as ballast in a racialized
world that could be hostile as well as nurturing, a world that,

though certainly challenging, was enlightened always with familial caring.

The seeds of this book were planted over numberless afternoons and evenings of storytelling around our dining room table (which was, not altogether anomalously, in the kitchen, where everything of importance happened). These are Day's stories, told and retold until they became mythic, growing roots that bound our family together in an extended organic system so deep and so wide that the recounting of the legends has never ceased. Her five children have continued relentlessly to tell the same stories to their own children. This memoir is nothing less than the stuff of who we know ourselves to be and to have always been; it traces our meanings backward and forward, following barely discernible clues of history. Our mother's stories have given us the maps by which our tribe locates its journeying, its streams and rivers, its stony places, its sometimes astonishing, more often incredibly affirming twists and turns.

We repeat these stories endlessly at family gatherings and say Amen to tales that carry the messages of survival and triumph. My one remaining brother, Arthur, raises his nearly six-foot-four frame from his chair like a preacher or a prophet, punctuating our childhood tales with broad, dramatic gestures and uncanny mimicry. My one remaining sister, Audrey, the baby of the family, brings to life my mother's last years with deadly accuracy, recalling in vivid and hilarious soliloquies how our mother's always sharp eye and tongue became like a rapier after she attained her eightieth year to heaven.

The importance of memory seeped into my consciousness very early. A somewhat odd child with few friends of my own age, I spent a great deal of time reading or talking to older people. I sat for hours listening to and learning from the grown-ups in my life: my teachers, the librarian, our playground instructors, the glamorous ladies downstairs who had danced on Vaudeville with Butterbeans and Susie, and the men from my father's lodge, the American Woodmen, who congregated in our living room on

Sunday afternoons and smoked cigars, drank bourbon, and told stories. I loved their high-spirited exaggerations and one-up-manship, the thrilling smoky masculinity of it all. The children in our family looked forward to the regular Sunday visits of those men, almost all of them post–World War I migrants from rural Louisiana, Mississippi, or Tennessee, and their tall tales were greeted with delight.

The best stories, though, were always our mother's. Because she was home every day when we came home from school, we spent untold hours in the kitchen with her, and while she was always deeply interested in what had happened to us that day, she often reflected on our chatter in terms of her own experience. She would sit and snap green beans or shell peas or fold or iron laundry or sew—this latter was endless work, because she had five active children. A talker and listener with a seven-track mind, our mother was never, never idle. She was a master of what is now called "active listening," and when she would ask, "What did your teacher have to say today?" she would help us along by weaving in at just the right places, "That reminds me of Mr. Grimes . . ." (her two-room schoolhouse teacher for what must have been six or eight years). Then she'd regale us with tales of Mr. Grimes' pedantry and pretensions, encouraging us to respect learning but always to see that everybody has a human side. Mostly she was teaching us to attend to our own experience, never to stand to the side of it. Because she cared so much, we did too. Simultaneously she was giving us an invaluable gift—that of understanding our parity in all situations, our right to assess for ourselves.

In our mother's world, her own children were extraordinarily gifted, of course. But she took even us with several grains of salt, just as she did our teachers, our doctors, our landlord, and our ministers and priests. The world was a serious enough place, but it was filled with laughter and good humor. She laughed at our funny traits, but we never felt devalued or even embarrassed because she laughed at her own too, and at those of our tall and prepossessing father and of her own well-beloved brothers. The only persons I never heard her laugh at were the three generations of powerful women who were her forebears. We heard dozens of stories about that triad: her great-grandmother Martha, always called Mamán; the storied Emmaline, the grandmother who helped to raise my mother and her two brothers; and their mother, Cornelia, known as Neeley, who died when our mother was only four years old. These special beings occupied a palpably different place in our lives, and we recognized this. We spoke of them always with solemnity.

When our mother was fifteen, her father was killed in a freak accident. A Southern aristocrat so profoundly identified with his British roots that he spoke of himself, and the surrounding community spoke of him, as "the Englishman," his death was an apocalyptic event in more ways than one. Deprived of his sure protection, our mother left all that she knew as home to follow the careful plan that he and Emmaline had made to ensure a more secure and more promising future for his daughter than life on the plantation would allow. Day was sent off to work as a live-in nursemaid for white friends of her father in New Orleans. There, our mother, in her blooming young womanhood, had her choice of paths. She could take her tenuous place in what was then called octoroon society, among other girls like herself whose bloodlines were mostly white (their one-eighth black blood was noted in the nomenclature). In this way she could "pass over the line" and live the remainder of her life in the white world, like many young women who shared her situation. Or she could find another way, looking white and living colored. Insisting on preserving what integrity and wholeness she could maintain, she chose the latter.

Our mother had grown to puberty in a multiracial context that, to an outsider, could seem crazily confusing. Within her family, however, what we now term identity problems never presented themselves. In the explicit and implicit life of the family, and in her own mind, terms such as *octoroon* or *mulatto* had little or no valence. Her British father, though responsible and caring, was prohibited from being a full-time, fully present male figure in her life by his allegiance to Southern mores. That was understood. Her mother, the illegitimate daughter of a German Jewish merchant and a mulatto woman, had died when she was a very small girl, so that the important lessons of her life, along with her most consistent emotional nurturance, had come from her colored extended family. That was also understood.

The few tales from our mother's early years are powerful stories, and ones that contain some essential clues to who she was, and therefore to who we are. Because I believe that we only understand our own histories as they are limned within the boundaries of our ancestors' lives, I am moved to write this memoir not only to unravel some of the mysteries, but also to honor those that must remain ambiguous. All histories are, of course, ineluctably fictional, the product of someone's imagination, the creation of some specific lens, and need to be recognized as such. My mother's stories themselves act, in this regard, as her fictions, although she would likely have railed at that idea. She was absolutely a straight shooter, not one to add unnecessary or elaborated detail: it was the bones of the story that were real to her, and although her voice is rich in the poetic prose of the South, the kind of easy exaggeration that was natural to my father was "nonsense" to her.

It is a source of enormous gratification to me and to my siblings that the Southern stories set forth here, including the most dramatic ones, were corroborated by researchers in the process of producing a potential documentary radio series based on my book. A production team including a genealogist and a cultural historian accompanied my siblings and me to the Mississippi/ Louisiana border region of our beginnings. With the help of local authorities, both black and white, they combed through mountains of material, locating old newspaper articles and birth and death records, letters and photographs at the Louisiana State Museum in Baton Rouge, and later, older records available through the Library of Congress. We all walked the overgrown paths of the plantation and conducted interviews with white and black citizens, relatives and neighbors, some nearly one hundred years old, who conveyed their uncannily sharp and detailed recollections. In some instances, they filled in the outlines with information previously unavailable to us. On a visit to a local synagogue, we found the photographs reproduced here of our mother's Jewish grandfather and his twin brother, both bearing a marked resemblance to a brown-skinned Shepherd cousin. At the local general store at the Pond, we found century-old books detailing the line of credit extended by that same forebear to his colored mistress, our great-grandmother Emmaline, confirming his reputation for financial responsibility within our family even as he continued as husband and father to his Jewish family down the road.

Although plans for the radio series failed to materialize, research material is integrated into these pages. Still, I choose to write down these stories mostly as passed on to us by our mother, acknowledging the vulnerability of this narrative, a mosaic of memory fragments glued together with my own latter-day imagination. I have taken occasional liberties in changing some names and some places.

Although it begins and ends with an intimate, personal event, this story of one particular mother takes on a larger importance because of its location within the wider history of what has appropriately been termed the American Century. At once personal narrative and sociohistorical document, this book may be read mostly as a collection of family stories inevitably anchored in the events of their time. I am fortunate that my mother's vivid oral recollection has afforded me the language and insight to illuminate the peculiar ironies and paradoxes of illegitimate intimacy between the races in the post-Reconstruction South.

Her African roots were tangled for generations with those of other forebears, German Jews and English Protestants and Irish Catholics, each tradition adding its historical richness. Her biography moves through a number of iconic moments and critical societal challenges. Her life was shaped not only by the New Orleans octoroon society phenomenon, but also by the conflicts and ingenuities of mulattoes negotiating Jim Crow discrimination; the Chicago race riots of 1919; the Great Depression and Prohibition as they affected urban "colored" life; the liberating implications of World War II and accompanying social mobility; the sweeping impacts of the civil rights movement; and, in her last decades, the emergence of fin de siècle African Americanism. Some of the experiences recorded here will strike a particular chord with people of color; some will speak most specifically to those from that part of the country known as the Deep South; others will have South Side Chicagoans of a certain age nodding yes in recognition. If I have been true to Day's voice and to the voices of our people, this narrative will invite readers into what William Blake called "the holiness of the minute particular" of a life that was in itself a truth-telling.

CHAPTER 1. *Alpha: The Long Mysterious Exodus of Death*

What we call the beginning is often the end
And to make an end is to make a beginning . . .
Every poem (is) an epitaph.

We shall not cease from exploration
And the end of all our exploring
Will be to arrive where we started
And know the place for the first time.

· T. S. ELIOT

One single drop of anything, blood on the water or cream in coffee, never tells the *whole* story. It might set you to thinking, but no way it can tell you the *whole* thing.

· MARTHA MONTGOMERY (MAMÁN)

June 10, 1986. The hospital room was cold, although summer had come early that year, and the clipped grass of the medical campus was that deep dense green that you usually wouldn't see in Chicago for another three or four weeks. Our brother Jay was present in spirit, and all four of our mother's surviving children were there that morning, exhausted and strained from a long night of waiting and drinking endless cardboard cups of metallic-tasting coffee, unalterably bitter no matter how many paper packets of sugar you added.

My brother Arthur was the only one in the family who didn't take his coffee black and scalding. He sat too, in his hospital greens, filling an empty carton with a dozen thimble-sized containers of half-and-half he had brought up from the cafeteria. I watched him peel away each foil circle with one thumb, our mother's unerring acuity in the clean motion of his meant-to-be-a-surgeon's hands. I watched the swirling circles of cream form on the surface of his coffee, a gradually slowing kaleidoscope, changing the coffee from nearly black to chocolate brown, then to café au lait and finally, just as the creamed coffee reached the brim, a rich ivory. Rhythms of color. We turned our coffee cups in our hands, simultaneously warming stiff fingers and performing the only purposive action we could think of. For over twenty-four hours now, we'd been sitting around our mother's bed watching her eighty-seven years of life on the earth come to an end.

That we were all there together was what she had asked for. Our mother didn't ask for much, not nearly as much as any of her children, certainly. We all wanted lots of things, summer houses and winter houses, large cars and Caribbean cruises, and all of us expected to see the world. All she ever explicitly said she wanted from life was three things: to live long enough to raise all of her own children (for she had been orphaned early); to maintain her mental balance ("to never lose my mind," is what she said); and finally, to have all of her children with her at the moment of her death. We used to tease her that this was too much to ask, especially this last thing, because she knew we all traveled so much.

We should have known that she would arrange it. Three days before she died, it became apparent that she was failing, and at first we took turns sitting with her, then on the day before, the ninth of June, on what would have been my father's eighty-sixth birthday and their sixty-second wedding anniversary, we made the decision to just stay with her, all of us. Arthur, born on

June 11, had silently spoken his personal request into the air: "Please Mother don't leave us on my birthday"; he didn't want that day to be indelibly shadowed with her passing. So our mother decided she could say goodbye on her own day. Just at dawn on June 10, with her three daughters and her one remaining son holding hands at her bedside, she breathed one last delicate breath and she was gone.

That is the only death I have ever witnessed, or hope to, and I was struck dumb by it. The parting of spirit and body was visible, a swift perceptible motion like a wind across her face, and then this uncanny stillness. Over a decade later, as I write, I reenter that awe-filled space. It is said, sometimes, that a person is "beautiful in death." Our mother truly was. Spared the kind of painful labored suffering that exhausts and diminishes the body, her clear skin and strong, elegant bone structure, maintained throughout her life, never left her. What was striking in death was not that, though, not just that clear core thing. That was perhaps anticipated. What surprised us was the profound tenderness in her face, an expression that all of her children knew from separate moments of maternal caring. She took one last breath, and there it was, that look. It was her legacy, exactly what she would want to leave us with, lest anybody forget that she was, first and last, a mother, consummate.

That much was clear. The rest was more complicated. That she died in the Catholic hospital where her grandson was a physician, though she was not and never wanted to be Catholic, had to be clarified, for the death certificate and all of the other papers. There was, too, the age question. One year older than my father, she had put her age back five years when they married, and none of us had found out until after he died, when the Social Security papers had to be filed. That was another thing to straighten out, for history. Then there was, inevitably, the race question. Whoever filled out the papers had looked at her and listed her race as white. One of us went to the thoroughly confused office staff and succeeded in getting the record set straight, only to find out from the funeral home people, who knew the family, that somewhere along the line the race had been revised once again to white. So she had to be changed, for perhaps the last time, back to black.

This peculiar peregrination, this swimming back and forth across so many established lines, seemed to me a metaphor for the way race and color, class and religion, had figured in our mother's life, with decisions and assumptions made by others creating a crosscurrent within which she had autonomously and stubbornly swum against the flow, creating her own unique place. To the end, all efforts notwithstanding, no one would really definitively draw a boundary around this woman. Like her father before her, she had made her own way, another way, and a lifetime of reflection on the layers of meaning in that way has culminated in the writing of this memory tale as homage and testament.

CHAPTER 2. *Beginnings:*
Strange Fates

When the stars self were young over Castries,
I loved you alone and I lived the whole world.
What does it matter that our lives are different?
Burdened with the loves of our different children? . . .
We here for one night. Tomorrow, the *Flight* will be gone.

· DEREK WALCOTT

Day's stories begin near the river, on the plantation everybody spoke of as the Place. I wanted to know about her father and mother and how these two might have come together in their unlawful conjunction. We have only the bare bones of the story, but we know the history of the Deep South, and we can imagine the two of them from faded photographs and bits of long-lost tales. The year it began was 1890, when both of them were not long past childhood.

At first Arthur, my grandfather, would have simply watched her, this girl Cornelia whom they called Neeley. It might have been her innate grace. The old sepia portrait that used to hang in our living room showed Neeley as a serious, almost somber young woman with light hair parted neatly in the middle and pulled back from a small heart-shaped face, her wide-set eyes accented by a high lace collar. They said she was different from the other girls around the Place. Her walk was unhurried, but measured and purposeful, her long legs seeming to know where they were going. Not that Arthur ever actually saw her legs; he saw only the ripple of fabric as she walked across his fields. But he knew, and she would have known that his eyes followed her.

When my grandmother was fifteen, the young master of Salisbury's five thousand acres began what might under other circumstances have been called a courtship. Three years older, he was already a square, stalwart young man, and she, just in the earliest bloom of womanhood. The old photos show him as somewhat thickset and not very tall. Still, fatherless from an early age, he walked his lands with the authority of inheritance and his mother's vested pride. The covey of nearly white young girls, Neeley and her two sisters, who lived down near the Pond were lively and interesting, and when Arthur tethered his horse near enough, they laughed and made pleasantries. That is, unless their Mamán was anywhere around. That eagle-eyed old woman kept a fierce watch over Neeley and all of her daughter Emmaline's brood as she sat bent over that old Singer, hour after hour, sewing sateen or chiffon dresses for some wedding on one plantation or another. The incessant clack-clack of her sewing machine would stop in a minute if she sensed danger to her own— and danger was hiding in their young girls' laughter as it carried into the house. These three girls of Emmaline's were choice— good looking every one, and proud, too, not holding their heads down for anybody. They attracted young men, white and colored, and either way, the situation had to be watched. Especially in the case of Arthur. She watched him watching Neeley, her daughter's firstborn, and she saw danger coming.

Neeley. He liked her name, even. I think he liked her quiet. She didn't laugh as much as the other, more carefree, sisters, but when she offered her slow smile, there seemed to be some new lightness about the Place. When he reflected on her, he could conjure up her wide, enigmatic grey eyes. In some way, people said, it was this peculiarly remote quality of hers that drew him to her. When it became obvious that she was his choice, the others would simply disappear when he rode up. After a time, compliant, she gave herself as a colored girl must when a rich white man staked a claim on her. But he would have understood vaguely that his power over her, although implacably embedded in the circumstance of that place and that time, had limits. And he'd be damned if he was going to allow that. With all of the Shepherd stubbornness, he committed himself to breaking through the thin-as-a-moth's-wing walls that kept them somehow apart even at the moments of their most profound intimacy.

When he walked about with her, the coloreds on the Place looked away, and the few white women looked down. His own white friends and overseers would have just smirked. Young Arthur was bold, they'd say that for him. Not that they would have picked out that one—her sisters promised more fun. And for sure he treated that Cornelia with a shade too much deference. That was dangerous, for him and for all of them, upsetting the order of things everybody understood. All of them hoped it would cool down. Especially his mother. Miz Katharine was kept informed by the old colored cooks who waited on her, and she didn't like the talk. In the earthy vernacular of rural people accustomed to the close observation of farm animals, the sassiest ones gossiped that Aunt Emmaline's oldest girl, the quiet one called Neeley, had opened young Arthur's nose. But none of them would have imagined a language of the heart, and the word *love* would not be spoken.

Miz Katharine watched carefully, but she thought it the better part not to say anything. She knew the young white boys often tried out the colored girls. That was almost a rite of passage for certain kinds of Southern boys, the hotheads, the arrogant, the showoffs. But it surprised her in Arthur, who had, she knew, a refined nature. She had sent him off to Sewanee, but he had implored her to let him come back home, and she had acceded. Perhaps that had been her mistake. She was troubled, now, by the new way he walked, with a certain loose-limbed ease she hadn't seen before. It occurred to her that perhaps she should send him up to her sister in Richmond for a while. But fate would not have her dilemma resolved so neatly, and when Miz Katharine finally suggested the trip, with an errand invented for that purpose, it was already too late. Unthinkably, the colored girl was breeding with his child, and he expressed his intention to build a house for her right there on the Place. Maternal tears, authentic or less so, could not dissuade this son of hers, who seemed to have up and lost whatever mind he had. Various threats were of no avail either. He was, after all, a young man, and she was an aging woman without a husband, and that Shepherd determination she had known in his poor dead father was what decided the whole thing. In the deceptive fairy-tale beauty of that deep South spring, on the plantation her husband had brought her to as a bride, her only living son worked his will, and everything was altered irrevocably.

Miz Katharine's thin lips tightened more each month as the house went up. Mercifully, her son had agreed to her request that the small, neat wooden house, with its four square rooms, each with two windows, be built on a far side of the Place where she didn't have to look at it or its inhabitants on a regular basis. She could sit anywhere on her veranda and not see it, although she couldn't get away from the sense of its growing presence, and the presence of this girl, Cornelia, who although she kept away from her sight as much as possible, was a living scandal on the Place.

Miz Katharine could not imagine what sin she was repaying by this daily tribulation. She had wanted desperately to return to Virginia after her husband died, and perhaps she had spent too many long days and nights railing against fate. Compelled to take on the burden of managing lands that never ceased to seem foreign to her, she had looked to Arthur to restore some peace to her last years. And now this. Her own stiff-necked pride wouldn't allow her to seek counsel from anyone they knew, and in the end, it seemed nothing could be done. All of Emmaline's household kept their distance, for which everybody on the Place was grateful. It wasn't the first time a colored girl had borne children by a gentleman . . . look at Emmaline's girls by one of those Jewish twins who ran the Pond Store, all of them so white they could pass . . . but Lord! Her own son getting caught up in *that* kind of net, putting that strange-eyed colored girl up in a house built expressly for her right there on their property, and her son walking out with the girl in broad daylight. Lord.

When the midwife and Dr. Brandon delivered Cornelia of the child, they had the audacity to give the boy, John, the Shepherd name. It was Arthur's firm decision, and there was no remedy for it. In the complexity of her predicament, Miz Katharine was torn between rage at her fate and a terrible curiosity to see the baby. A bastard octoroon boy with her son's—my Lord, even her *own*—blood running in his veins.

It seemed as though a shadow passed over the sun when Arthur asked if he could bring the boy to her. That was unthinkable, and she had no trouble telling him so. Still, as the days lengthened, that Neeley or another of Emmaline's girls would walk the baby in the afternoon, and one day she set eyes on him across the field. One can almost see her hand fly to her throat— that bastard baby boy, the spit and image of his father, without one mark of the Negro anywhere on him. Strangely chilled, Miz Katharine would have turned away and walked swiftly into her own house, closing the door behind her. She would have taken dinner in her room and claimed the flu for the next three days. By the time she emerged, she would have resigned herself.

The girl Neeley lost two babies in a row after that, growing quieter and frailer each time. But the small boy they called Bully—he was named John Turnbull after somebody on the English side—was the delight of his father. Arthur himself seemed to grow up nearly overnight, shedding his boyish awkwardness and turning into a clear-eyed, serious man. To Miz Katharine's despair, her son carried his boy about on his shoulders, put him on a pony and walked him over the fields, or sat shamelessly on the steps of the Small House reading stories to him. She had absolutely forbidden Arthur from taking that boy off the Place. She first commanded and then implored her son to please not take the child up to Natchez or to any of the other plantations, reminding him of the lack of safety, the bad water, the rampant malaria fever. She didn't mention her deadliest fear, the one that sometimes took hold of her in the middle of the night, when she would awaken trembling. What if some gang of rednecks who had heard the rumors might hurt him? Arthur seemed completely unaware of any potential danger to him or the boy. But he had to know things happened down there. The dense trees concealed things. They had all heard stories. And so she prayed without ceasing that no harm would come to her child over this Negro folly, and was quietly grateful each time she learned of one of Cornelia's miscarriages.

When the boy called Bully was three years old, that poor frail Cornelia had a girlchild, and this one survived. Miz Katharine dreaded the possibility that her son might actually dare to give the child her name, and she was profoundly relieved when this did not occur. The child was named Thelma, after one of the coloreds down to Longmont, a friend of Emmaline's girls who visited them from time to time. This time, Miz Katharine marched right into the Small House and looked upon her son's daughter, who, like her brother before her, looked for all the world like a white baby. But gratefully she did not resemble the Shepherds. She didn't look much like that strange-eyed Cornelia, either. Rather, she had a round face and dark hair, harkening back to the Montgomerys, really very much a tiny, finer featured version of Emmaline herself. Irrationally calmed for the moment, Miz Katharine turned on her heel, leaving word with the sisters to let her know if Cornelia needed anything. Surprising herself, she recognized that this time was definitely different. She had become inured to the oddity of her son's decisions and to the fragility of their predicament.

One year later, the girl Cornelia would produce a final son for her Arthur, this one to be named Benjamin Berthold, after the absent father of Emmaline's girls. Everybody on the Place knew about him, that German Jew up the road with the fancy behaviors who had been so taken with Emmaline, causing a shameful scandal for his family. That thing between them went on long enough to produce those three white-looking, cat-eyed girls, one right after the other, and finally the one boy, before his twin brother, Karl, pressured him to move his poor scandalized German wife and their little children away to New Orleans, and after that any talk of him just disappeared from the life on the Place. His name didn't disappear, though. Although Emmaline carried the Montgomery name to her death, all of the children she bore for that man were Lehmanns from the start. Emmaline's one son, Jacob, disappeared too, and they said he had been sent to live with other family somewhere farther north. People speculated that his father had sent him to some Jewish orphanage or something like that, because nobody ever wanted to talk about him and he never came back Down Home. Now along came Cornelia's second boy, this one greatly resembling that Jewish side of his lineage, sharp blue eyes and all, and she gave him a German name after those people. They called him Ben for short, and he didn't look in any way a Shepherd, up one side or down the other. Her son never took to him the way he had that first bastard boy.

Then before any of these three could even make their First Holy Communion, that fated Cornelia took her leave of this world in yet another childbirth, but this time she took her last newborn with her to the grave, a girlchild, unnamed, and buried right there with her mother. Emmaline would take on the raising of all three of Arthur's children right there behind her house, and Miz Katharine would grow old there on the Place, with those colored children at her back, and everything out in the open like that. She would pray without ceasing.

CHAPTER 3 . *Sacred Wounds*

Promised immortality,
what we are wanting is a Sign.

What we are wanting is some word
on the wind or on the water,
some finger-of-God bylined miracle,
some opening
in the great silence.

Promised immortality,
what we are wanting is a Sign.
What we are given is a History
conjugated in the blood

· RONNE HARTFIELD

I spent long hours with my mother in her waning years.
On occasion, I slept overnight, lying beside her in bed, the two
of us talking into the night until she fell asleep. She loved to talk
about the old days, and when I asked her to describe her very
earliest memory, this is the way she responded:

*If I had been old enough to have any words to talk about it the way I
can now, I'd have said for sure I had a premonition. As it was, what I
remember is that I felt feverish and weak that morning, and the old people*

scolded me because I pushed my breakfast away. That just-before-sick feeling didn't leave me all day. My eyes were hot and just heavy, and I remember my legs felt heavy, too, and I didn't want to leave the house. My mama was feeling poorly herself, and so the old people took me away down to the Pond, telling me my sweet tired mama didn't need a fussy little girl around, and besides I might have a new baby before the day was out—maybe a sister this time. That should have pacified me—I felt shut out sometimes being just in the middle of two brothers, one older and one younger than me, and it might be a really good thing if I had a sister. But that day, just nothing was making me feel better. The damp, steamy air at the Pond felt heavy too, and when I waded, the skirt-tail of my yellow dress—I remember it was yellow—got wet, and that made me feel heavy from top to bottom.

Then, late in the afternoon at the hottest part of the day, Great-Aunt Calline and Lil Aunt Nettie came to get me. They took me away home to stand at the head of my mama's bed, and one thing that still makes me sad is that I don't even remember how she looked, just how her voice sounded. She always spoke quiet anyway, but she was really quiet that day. Everybody for miles around loved Mama the best of all her sisters because she was the quietest and sweetest-tempered of all of them.

Aunt Irene, the one next to my mama, had a quick, sharp tongue and was in our lives a lot because she never had any children of her own. The middle sister, Aunt Sarah, had eight children who were almost like brothers and sisters to me, and she just seemed worn out all the time. Some of her girls had spirit and I liked being with them. Lil Aunt Nettie was the youngest, and a mean-mouth, worse than even Aunt Irene. People said the reason she was the meanest had something to do with the facts: first of all, she was an afterthought; then, she was the worst-looking of the sisters, and wore a rag tied around her head because she didn't have pretty hair like the other girls. In the long run, Lil Aunt Nettie outlived all of the rest, which she herself predicted. She used to say she would live to be a hundred because she was born on the dark side of the moon. My own mother, Cornelia, they called her Neeley, was their family's beauty spot, with wide-set grey eyes and beautiful long hair that she would let me comb. I had long hair, too—when I was very small it reached all the *way down my back and Mama praised me for it. With two rough boys, she liked having a little girl to fuss over. Mamán always said she would spoil me for life.*

That day, I remember that when I stood by her bed she kept touching my hair with her hands, pushing it out of my eyes, and she just kept looking at me so strange. It made me feel hot and funny, and like I knew I was supposed to act some way that I did not know how. My mama, who they called Neeley, touched my hair so soft and what she said to me was that now I would have to learn to be a woman. Then they held me up to kiss her and took me out of the house. That was the last I ever saw of my mama. She bled to death that hot afternoon lying stretched out on the very bed I was born in. The bedsheets and pillowcases were soaked through with my mama's blood, and I can still shut my eyes and see the scarlet stain of it, even when I can't see her face at all. You all may make light of it, because I was just a little child, but I never stop wishing I had committed my mama's face to memory that heavy day.

My newborn little sister died that same day too, they told me. That year, nineteen hundred and three, my mother, Neeley, was twenty-seven years old. I was four. The childbed fever was a danger then and it still is for women. After all those years I worry myself to death every time one of my own daughters goes into labor. When you have daughters that go down, as we say, you'll know. As women, we are all bound up in the same thing. It's a woman's thing, and it's just there for us, the hard bearing of children, the scare you can't get away from that comes with the long waiting, and all of that blood.

CHAPTER 4. *On the Place*

Occasionally the river floods these places, but in fact it is not
flooding; it is remembering. Remembering what it used to be.
All water has a perfect memory and is forever trying to get back
to where it was. . . . It is emotional memory, what the nerves and
the skin remember as well as how it appeared. And a rush of
imagination is our flooding.

· TONI MORRISON

*This is how it was. People worked down there. Children, too,
when they were not in school, and our school year was nowhere near as
long as yours. Some people worked in the fields, planting or picking cotton, harvesting cane or sorghum. Our people didn't do too much of that.
Mostly, they worked around the Big House, keeping things up inside and
out. Everybody knew my father's mother Miz Kate was a taskmaster
woman. She didn't like to see anybody resting themselves for more than
one minute. And she liked her silver shining and her mahogany tabletops
polished to a T, so it took a lot of people just to see to that work in all
those different rooms. She had my great-uncle Frank as her carriage man,
and he had to keep the horses and saddles just so, which provided work for
some of the other men too. Then there was the gardening and the laundry
work and the cooking. Great-Aunt Calline was the main overseer of the
inside work, which was the right job for* her *because she was a taskmaster woman herself. It was her nature, and anybody could see that she liked
nothing better than telling people what to do. One reason she never was*

too fond of me was that she couldn't tell me what to do. Mamán herself told me I didn't have to mind Aunt Calline, because I was a motherless child and the only people with permission to chastise me were herself and Mama Emmaline.

My father did come around at pretty regular times. I didn't look forward to it, though my cousins thought I should, because he always brought me presents, a new dress or shoes, a doll with fancy clothes, a picture book. There was a reason why his coming to our house was not a cause for celebration on my part, and it was this: he asked too many questions, and if I didn't answer just the way he thought I should, he would be stern with me, and with Mama Emmaline too, frowning at her that I should be taught this or that. Mamán would dress me up and tie my hair up with ribbons when he was coming over, and I never did like to be fussed over, even when I was a little girl. Then the boys would go over with me what I had learned in school and so forth. They wanted to please him, but I didn't care so much about that. They loved it when my father came, and he would end up patting them on the back and giving them spending money. But me—he would correct my English, tell me not to be such a tomboy, and then kiss me on both cheeks, which I didn't like too much either.

As I grew older, I didn't mind him as much. It seemed I met up with his expectations more, and he allowed as how I was becoming a tolerable young lady. Plus he promised that he would see to it that I could go to New Orleans soon, when I attained my proper young ladyhood. That was the object of my ambition, and I was absolutely dying to go. I bragged to my cousins that my father was going to have me driven to the city in one of his phaeton carriages, and that made them furious, except for Irene, who I promised to ask if she could go with me instead of one of the boys. Mama Emmaline said she would work on it.

After my poor mama died, Mama Emmaline took over things at our house, and just taking care of us was what she did. She kept us immaculate, or at least we would start out that way. We had to wash ourselves in the mornings—my brother John would draw water from the cistern and fill our big zinc tub, and we would take turns washing ourselves. I was first, being the only girl. We had a big breakfast every day, and when school was in session, we walked over there. It wasn't too far, and I loved the walk with my brothers.

All the children in our little colored school looked up to us because of our father and because my brothers had a reputation for being people you didn't mess around with. I was very good with my lessons, and our teacher, Mr. Grimes, was crazy about me because he liked a person to speak up and I never had any trouble with that. Our school had two rooms, one for the little children and one for the older. We had seat work and recitations, and singing too. We didn't go home at midday but took a lunch pail and sat outside with that. My playmates were usually the Lehmann girl cousins, Winifred, Nettie, Precious, Truelove, and Irene, my favorite. Their brothers, Lee, John, and Willie Edward, were always fun, too, gamemakers every one. My brother Ben stayed around with them, but our brother John was too much older to spend too much time with that bunch. He had a few friends of his own, but kept to himself a lot of the time, unless he was spending time with our father.

Our father had a big part in raising John. He went riding about with him, over to his other plantations. He was the one who taught John how to keep accounts, and he brought him books and papers which they would have long conversations about. The one thing he still had to do was to keep John away from Miz Kate. We knew she had caused big trouble for my father when he built our house, and even more so when he put up the second house next door to us for Aunt Sarah Lehmann and her children to occupy. Mamán loved to tell the story about how Miz Kate had insisted that our houses be far enough behind the Big House so she wouldn't have to see us going back and forth. Mamán would imitate Miz Kate throwing up her hands and saying "Oh Ah-thur, if it is your unchangeable will to do this disgraceful thing, then you must have a path cut on the far side of the Place, beyond my sight." And our father did that, and we had our own little road, so we could take another way home and never had to walk the wide Oak Allée that led up to the Big House. We were glad we didn't have to go the regular way—it was almost like we had our private little world back our way, with all of the people who mattered to us, our own garden, and our own judgment on what happened on the Place.

We kept up with everything, because Mamán was the one everybody on the Place came to talk to all the time. Besides that, Mama Emmaline was the main fancy seamstress for miles in any direction, so white people who had money came to make arrangements about their party dresses or wedding dresses or whatever, and when they came, they talked. Our house was always full of talk. We heard the good things, like when some smart young person on the Place got to go up to Tuskegee Institute or Tougaloo College, and we heard the bad things too, though most of that was told in whispers—when the Klan was riding, when some colored man got shot up or worse for speaking out too smartly. It was times like that when Mama Emmaline would tell us we were lucky we didn't have to worry about anybody bothering us because of our father. Still, our father saw to it that John was taught early how to shoot, and we had rifles in the house.

I had decided to be a seamstress myself because that was a respected occupation and Mama Emmaline had taught me well—I mastered that Singer sewing machine before I was ten years old. Our father thought I should go to school and become a nurse, maybe up North. That seemed like it might be a good idea, too, because I was good at taking care of people, being the only girl. Plus, being brought up with one brother on either side of me I didn't scare easy, and our father could be brought to laugh out loud when somebody reported on how I had taken up a stick and killed a coach-whip snake on the road to Edgefield. He wanted me to be a young lady, but not a timid one. He was a Shepherd, and after all was said and done, so was I.

CHAPTER 5. *Matriarchy*

Child
what are you wishing? What pact
are you making?
What mouse runs between your eyes? What ark
Can I fill for you when the world goes wild? . . .
Child, I cannot promise that you will get your wish.
I cannot promise very much
I promise you love. Time will not take away that.

· ANNE SEXTON

Although we learned our mother's entire history, gradually and nonchronologically, the earliest years remain shrouded
in considerable mystery, somehow laden with a gravity entirely
unlike the rest of her life after she went north. Because of this,
there are only a few stories from the first decade or so of the life
written down in these pages. What we know is that between the
ages of five and fifteen, Day Shepherd developed into a quite remarkable young woman. After the untimely death of my young
grandmother, Neeley, my mother and her two brothers occupied the same small house they had been born in, nurtured with
unswerving love and discipline by their mother's mother, the
fabled Emmaline, and their great-grandmother, Martha Montgomery, their adored Mamán.

The power inherent in this double matriarchy was the loamy stuff of my mother's beginnings. Her grandmother, Emmaline, was a strong, proud woman who had reared four girls without much visible sustenance from any man. The oldest girls, Cornelia, Sarah, and Irene, were full-blooded sisters who bore the name Lehmann, in this way acknowledged by their Jewish father, of whom they spoke as Mister Berthaw, bloodline intimacies notwithstanding. Besides the name, there appeared to be little accountability for them beyond the establishment of an open line of credit at the general store he and his twin brother owned.

These financial arrangements might have come to an end with Berthold's marriage to a German immigrant woman, well after his relationship with Emmaline had begun, but the records confirm that the line of credit continued even after Berthold Lehmann had moved his legitimate family to New Orleans, and, indeed, the line of credit existed on the books at the Pond Store until Emmaline's death. Nonetheless, even with the modicum of security afforded her by this arrangement, Emmaline would undoubtedly have been vulnerable to many of the hardships that afflicted so many colored women in her circumstance without the resourcefulness of her Mamán, a respected and protected house servant and seamstress of legendary talents. As it was, things were not easy. She lived in Mamán's house, adding a new baby girl nearly every year for a while, including the last one, whom people whispered about. They said Nettie, the last girl, was the unhappy price of one hot night when Emmaline had walked out alone and a local colored man had grabbed her. This story was never verified, but it was a visible fact that this dark-skinned girl came from a different father, and she bore a different surname, Jolla. It was also clear that her mother was always more protective of this Nettie than of the other girls. Certainly Berthold Lehmann was not present in the home life of his little female family on the Place. With his legal German Jewish wife and several children, B. B., along with his twin brother, was active in the temple upriver in Natchez. Obviously the close-knit, insular Jewish community would have known of B. B.'s illegitimate family, but everyone involved turned their faces away for years, and after the recognized family moved away to New Orleans, he opened another store there, became active in Jewish life, and did not return to the Pond.

The one son Emmaline had borne him, a blue-eyed boy named Jacob, disappeared from the Place very early on. Although people whispered that the baby's father had secreted him away somewhere with some Jewish people in New Orleans, this was never verified. The census records from the 1920s, to which we gained access much later, do show one Jacob Lehmann living as a white man in New Orleans. In any case, at some point Jake Lehmann appears to have made a decision to move to Chicago, where he lived as a colored man, though he always passed for white in his profession as a carpenter. In the North, he married a mulatto woman, raised a family, and managed to acquire a good deal of property on the city's South Side before reuniting with the children of his sisters.

Over the years, Emmaline and Mamán became something of a force in the surrounding area. It was therefore not entirely surprising that after Neeley died Emmaline was called upon for help by the young master of the Place. He had taken good care of her poor frail daughter Neeley until she gave out birthing yet one last child for him, and that last one was buried right in the ground with her. In grief spoken of as entirely unsuitable for a man of his position, Arthur Shepherd had asked Emmaline to come and live in the house he had built for Neeley and his children and to raise them with his support. Experienced in the ways of that time and place, she proposed a shrewd bargain: she would come on condition that he would put up an adjacent second house for her other husbandless daughter, Sarah, who had several children fathered by an irresponsible Irish friend of the Shepherds, a cold, bone-thin man who had never done much to help them and never gave the children his name. In immediate need of someone to care for his three children, my grandfather agreed more or less readily, and for all of the following years until the end of his life, he helped to sustain both households, assuring a viable future for Mamán and all of her progeny.

The stories of those years confirm my mother and her brothers' sense of being carefully protected from a potentially hostile world. They were aware that their white grandmother, the haughty Miz Kate, found their very presence on the Place a constant threat to her peace of mind. But as much as she wished they would disappear into thin air—or at least to New Orleans where mulattoes abounded—her son took a visible pride in his children, joining Mamán and Emmaline in their praise for school achievements.

The regular Friday afternoon recitations at their tiny country colored school were occasions for the children to shine. Each of the Shepherd children perfectly committed to memory each week a multiverse poem of Edgar Allan Poe ("Annabel Lee") or William Wordsworth ("Thy soul was like a Star, and dwelt apart: / Thou hadst a voice whose sound was like the sea" or "I wandered lonely as a cloud / That floats on high o'er vales and hills"), or the rousing declarations of Leigh Hunt ("Abou Ben Adhem [may his tribe increase!] / Awoke one night from a deep dream of peace") or John Greenleaf Whittier ("No longer forward nor behind / I look in hope or fear; / But, grateful, take the good I find / The best of now and here"). In the last decades of her life my mother would, to my delight, recite these pieces in their entirety, in the dramatic cadence of a Louisiana schoolgirl.

Day could memorize poems, yes, but she could also ride horses bareback, her long dark hair flying behind her. She learned to help Mamán keep house, each thing in its proper place, work accomplished with discipline and orderliness. She learned fine sewing from Emmaline and by age twelve could make her own clothes. Day also learned early to cook. She planned and prepared superb meals, and the garden she tended put forth prodigiously, crisp peas and peppers, sweet-smelling bridal wreath and brightly colored zinnias and what my mother called four o'-clocks. Not close to her father like her older brother was, or to Mama Emmaline the way her younger brother was, she was a bit of a loner. Feeling her singularity, she spent a lot of time with Mamán and learned to enjoy the certain unique place she occupied in her world.

Day was growing into herself. Stubborn like the Shepherds, candid and resourceful like the Montgomerys, devoted to family like the Lehmanns, she developed a fiercely independent core entirely her own. Her brothers had their own bonding, and her Aunt Sarah's girls had each other. At times she was allowed into their female circle, but when she excelled beyond them at school or on horseback, the Lehmann cousins would exclude her, taunting her with the chant "motherless child, motherless child." Half a century later, my mother's eyes would cloud over with recollected pain. She would encircle in her arms whichever of us was near and say, "You must always cherish one another. Let nothing or no one come between you." "People will try to pit you against each other," she would say, and she was right, too. "But you must always know that your *own* are yours until the end, and that blood is thicker than water. I was motherless, so I had to be strong, and then, before I could grow up entire, I was fatherless too. You were never motherless children, and your family is your strength."

At fifteen, Day was a self-described "moon-fixer," meaning she was tall for the times. She was a fierce, hazel-eyed octoroon beauty growing into her young ladyness, and the boys, both white and colored, were beginning to take notice. She would walk with her cousins the several miles over to Fort Adams for ferry rides on the river, and learning to tame a bit of her tongue, she was preparing herself for whatever the future might bring. And then, without warning, her father's life was cut shockingly short. This proved to be an apocalyptic event in more ways than one, and I write it here nearly exactly as she told it. It was a turning point in her life and became a mythic event in our family history.

CHAPTER 6. *The Lightning Fields*

Human life . . . is a vale of soulmaking . . . *soul* as distinguished
from intelligence—(individuals) are not *souls* till they acquire
identities, till each one is personally itself. . . . How, but by the
medium of a world like this?

· JOHN KEATS

After that August of the lightning, so many things
would never be the same again. First of all, it was *really* hot that
fateful summer, the air so stagnant and thick that everything
went into slow motion, cooks in the kitchen, children in the
yard, barn animals, even the sticky leaves in the sorghum fields.
That's the way our mother remembered it, anyway, and that's
the way people talked about it for a long time afterward. Second
of all, this was 1913 in the Deep South river country, walking
distance from the border of Mississippi and Louisiana. People
were already upset because of the gathering talk of the conflict
overseas, feeling what would be called Woody Wilson's War
slowing its way toward them, and they dreaded any idea of so
many of their boys being taken all that way across the Atlantic
Ocean to fight against foreigners, called upon against their will
to try out their honor against the Kaiser, whoever he was. Vicksburg was just up the road, and you could still talk to people who

lived right there at the battlefield and remembered the sound of the guns.

Hundreds of brave Southern boys had gone down in glory at Vicksburg, fighting their hearts out under Admiral Pemberton and turning away Grant's Yankees not once but twice before they were finally overcome. There is a stone marker right in the center of Fort Adams, where people still board the ferry to ride downriver to New Orleans. It's carved with the names of all the Wilkinson County boys lost in that battle, and white people around there were still in grief over those boys, over the loss to their families and the loss of what they called the Southern Way of Life. The coloreds had a different eye on it, of course, not sharing in the general lament. They talked among themselves about Vicksburg and the whole War of Liberation, and to their way of thinking, General Grant's whipping the Johnny Rebs at Vicksburg had been a great day. Some of the older colored people had taken to memory President Abraham Lincoln's entire proclamation, the one that should have set the thing to rest once and for all. Abe Lincoln had a way with words a lot of the time, they thought—he looked like a preacher and sounded like one too, and what he said about Vicksburg and about their own Old Man River sounded straight out of the Good Book. What he had actually said was that "The Father of Waters," meaning the Mississippi, of course, "can again go unvexed to the sea." The situation they lived with was not so unvexed as all that, but everybody, white and colored alike, shared in this one resolution: yes, the War of the States may have meant different things to different races, but there wasn't one single family that was not relieved when the war was finally over and people could get back to living their ordinary lives.

And now while people still alive were still remembering everything about the War Between the States, they could feel in their bones the slow gathering clouds of another kind of war to deal with, and most people didn't understand why Southern boys, colored and white, might be yanked off the plantations *again,* leaving so many mothers without sons and young wives without husbands. Stories grew that way in that place, the public became the personal and vice versa, with people putting their stories together, collectively reshaping their shared and separate times. In that way, this new war growing around them that they were never to name as their own weighed on them like the heat all that summer, turning their spirits heavy and sodden. Instead of peace and quiet there on the Place, everybody's nerves got more on the edge. As children sat on the steps of the Small Houses, their voices grew more shrill, and in the barns the cows lowed interminably, resting on their haunches while the phaeton-carriage horses stood stock-still and rolled their eyes crazily at each other. And Miz Katharine—well, she got meaner. Miz Katharine was trouble most of the time anyway. But, my mother said, when the bad heat came you had to leave that old lady by *herself.*

That Tuesday afternoon, Miz K sat heavily on the big house veranda and fanned herself. She was my father's mother, a Virginia lady, and she was too proud or too fancy to use regular church fans, saying that she had no intention to advertise anybody's burial parlor. Rather, she kept her own special rose-colored lace fan close to hand. Somebody had brought it to her from overseas. That particular day, Miz Katharine was sitting there in her big old wicker chair with the green flowered cushions, fanning away with that rose-colored fan of hers, frowning at nothing or everything, when suddenly the air changed. You know from your own experience that it does that down there sometimes. In the middle of a long slow stillness, the earliest sense of a storm will make itself felt without any warning you can name. It's not the wind exactly. More of a prickling in the ears and the nose, like before you sneeze. That particular day, it didn't get cool, as people testified, but the air took on some kind of motion, just barely there but there, *and a giant-sized zigzag of lightning out of nowhere flashed across the sky. "A good thing," Miz Katharine said. "Some rain is what's needed." Her son's crops needed it. She liked to watch storms anyway. Mamán said that without a husband around, that old woman had to take her excitement when she could get it.*

Mamán herself did not like storms. She had a bit of African remembrance in her still, and thought in some hoodoo kind of way that big lightning and thunder meant God had his teeth on edge with somebody or something. So when lightning came, with that sky-breaking crack of thunder following on its tail, all the children came inside and found something to do with themselves so as not to pay too much attention to the storm coming at them. It was a little scary even if you didn't have too much African mind about yourself. That day it was truly fearsome, because the sky turned such strange colors. One minute it was blue-blue, like a wildflower, heavy and so slow-feeling you could almost feel the thickness. Then the lightning came, sudden as first blood down a girl's thigh when she turns into her womanhood. And then the light changed, just like that, from blue-blue to a kind of sick-looking green with streaks of red in it. It just got darker until it was almost night-black, and all the while there'd come these lighted-up flashes and boom-boom sounds, cracking open the thick quiet all across the Place. The hard rain that soaked everything out there was an afterthought, really.

People had different ideas about the time of day, but it seemed to have been somewhere in the late afternoon, because nobody was thinking about supper yet. Miz Katharine just sat out there on her wicker chair and watched it all, not caring that everybody with any sense had gone inside. She did leave off from fanning though, and started up humming the way she did when she thought nobody could hear her. The funny part was, she would hum colored people's songs, church songs that her cooks sang in the kitchen. She just took those songs to memory without thinking about it. If she had thought about it, you can bet she surely wouldn't have learned those songs. She did not like to have any more to do with the coloreds than she had to just to keep the Place going.

Because the air was so strange, those tunes moved right through the space in between the Big House and the Small Houses, and all of the people heard her humming, and some of the old people started to sing the words themselves. Not Mamán, though. She didn't sing. What she remembered was the humming. Aunt Calline remembered the song as one of those Lord-Jesus-help-me songs, and Lil Aunt Nettie remembered exactly, she said, that the song Miz K was humming was "Way Down Yonder by Myself and I Couldn't Hear Nobody Pray." You couldn't argue with Lil Auntie about things like that, so that just became everybody's recollection.

Anyway, that humming was the last sound people remembered coming from out of Miz Katharine's thin tight lips for the next three days. After Mr. Miles, our father's colored foreman, came riding up on his horse with a face nobody would ever forget, streaking wet with rain and crying, even though grown men didn't cry in that part of the world, to carry the news to that mean humming woman, she never spoke a word for the next three days. The news was this: that her only son, our father, had been struck dead by lightning, sitting on his horse Rafe, under a tree.

Miz Katharine Shepherd didn't say one word when that message was brought to her by Mr. Miles, whose life had been spared because of this rule: No colored person could get under a tree when a white man was there seeking shelter. So Mr. Miles had been on his own horse, some distance from the persimmon tree that drew the lightning, and he just got soaking wet. Now he actually got down off his own horse, crying, and then walked fast up the steps to where she was sitting and got down on bended knee carrying that heavy news to my father's mother.

People said Miz K almost died on the spot, and that it was her heart that broke in two inside her body that stopped her windpipe from moving so that she couldn't speak any words at all that frightful night. They thought with the whole place in such terrible grief, people running all over every which way, repeating the news over and over to anybody they could find, that the words to speak might come back to Miz Katharine in a rush and that she would run across the field screaming out the name of her only son, screaming against God or screaming for some kind of help from Jesus, but she didn't. She got up from her wicker chair and turned into the house she lived in with her son, and she walked into her room and lay down on that big walnut bed, the same one she slept in by herself every night of her life except when she went to visit her sister's family back in Virginia. People talked about how she turned her head to the wall and never let loose one word for three days, even after the sun came back out. She never got up to view her only son's body, which had been brought in by his foreman. Not even after the white burial parlor people had laid him out on a cooling board in the back visiting room, where he lay looking perfect and just like he always did except with his eyes closed.

Word got around about two strange things. One was about that: Arthur Shepherd, laid out as he was, looked so untouched, *like he was just sleeping, not black and blue from being knocked off Rafe's back by that bolt of lightning—not a lightning burn on him anywhere you could see. People pondered what that occurrence might mean. Some old people on the Place said that the man must have been taken up by an angel. This was because he was known to be a* good *white man, good to us three colored children who bore his name, not hiding anything from anybody, and he had built us our little house on the Place, close enough so he could walk over and visit us when he wanted to. He was pretty good to the people who worked for him too. Because his people had come from England and he had a cousin over there named* Sir Henry Hook Shepherd *and everybody knew about* that, *and because he spoke softly and different from the other high-toned white people around, even differently than his mother, who just had a Virginia whiny-in-the-nose manner of talking, most people agreed that he was a* good *white man.*

Still, Lil Auntie herself never did like him much. She said he wasn't really all that free-handed, and that you had to really make yourself a case *to get something if you needed it, so it was clear as day to her that he wasn't taken up by any angel. She said she had heard before of other people, white and black, good and bad people, who got struck down by lightning and ended up with not a mark on them. But there were a lot of the shout-in-church-type people on the Place, the ones that Lil Auntie and Mamán said you should keep a little distance away, handling them with a long-handled fork. Those kinds of people still said that good man's spirit was taken up into those big dark rain clouds by an angel, no doubt about it, so quite naturally his remains looked perfect.*

The second strange thing was that Miz Katharine would not listen to anybody tell her how it happened, how her son had been riding across his own fields when the rain came down, and he had stopped under a tree no different than he had done a hundred times before, except this time this one streak of lightning just aimed itself right at him, cutting through that old persimmon tree like a strop-sharpened knife. Everybody wanted to tell her their version, but Miz K just kept her head turned to the wall, and if people would come in she would throw up her hands like the colored people do when they're saying "Lord Have Mercy," but she didn't say the words, just put up her hands, and people would leave her alone out of respect or fear. Some people thought she had gone silent crazy like Miz Louann down at the Pond, or like Miz Rachel over to Longmont, and wouldn't ever talk again. The coloreds on the Place were more than a little scared of any kind of crazy white people, especially when you didn't know what they might do if they came to.

While she was still in her silent grief, all of Miz Katharine's relatives came streaming in from Virginia, where they had named a whole town after the Shepherds over a hundred years ago. The whole place seemed almost like a party, with so much coming and going and cooking and men drinking, and heaps of flowers everywhere, arrangements of Broken Wheels and Bleeding Hearts and Flowering Crosses of all different sizes. But it was not a party, and the white burial parlor people were there every day, making arrangements for a really big funeral without any instructions from Miz Katharine. That lady had long before written out her will and last testament, and left a copy of her handwritten directions for her own funeral service, express written out selections for hymns and prayers for her own funeral, all while she was still alive. She had left the whole list with Lawyer Bramlette on her sixtieth birthday. That's the kind she was. No colored person would ever invite the attention of Death that way, and a lot of white Christian people wouldn't either. But anyway, they used those directions to put together a funeral for my father, fitting for a man as important as her son, a man whose family had owned seven plantations up and down the Natchez Trace and all the way alongside the river down to New Orleans, who got struck down when he was only forty-one years old and surely Death hadn't crossed his mind yet.

The big question was, could Miz Katharine be roused back to speech for the funeral of her only son? Well. Something or another got to her, and, waking up on the funeral morning, still silent as a spook, she all at once came back to herself. She got up and washed and put up her hair and put on a long heavy black dress. Then she put a hat on her head and drew a net-veil over her face, which was as white as an onion under that veil, with its black specks like pockmarks dotting her cheeks and chin. People knew every detail because, of course, the colored maids were the ones to help her get dressed. Those gossiping house-Negroes attained greater im-

portance than they had ever had or expected to have, because they and only they could tell the real story, and everybody was dying to hear it all.

All of those coloreds who worked in the Big House, the cooks and the carriage drivers too, half of them our family, filed into the big double parlor, which was all set up with chairs, and took their places at the rear, behind the distant family, friends, neighbors, and everybody else who was white, and behind Mamán and Mama Emmaline and us three children, dressed in our best. I had a ribbon pinned to my hair because I never did like the way I looked in my Sunday hat. Miz Wilkie from down near Longmont Plantation played the rosewood piano, one sad-sounding white hymn after another, and everybody sat in their seats, leaving the first three rows free and empty so when Miz Katharine walked in with her sister and her nieces and nephews, she wouldn't have to brush up against anybody's knees or trip over anybody's long funeral dress. Then came my father's sister, Miz Margaret, who had had a falling out with Miz Katharine a long time ago, over something people clicked tongues about. That one had moved way up north of Natchez and never had come back until this day, so people were entirely interested in her, and surprised that she looked pretty much the same. Then came some other family members from Natchez, from New Orleans, and from Virginia.

When Miz Wilkie finally broke into "In Heavenly Love Abiding," our father's other family on the Place came walking in lock-step, like in a wedding procession. Miz Louise, the strange silent woman Miz K had brought down from Kentucky for our father to marry after our mother died and who never talked much to Miz K or anybody else, marched her three little children directly up to the front across the aisle and sat all of them down, staring straight ahead. Mamán had told us that Miz Louise had been sent for and put before our father because Miz K was determined that he should have what she called "legitimate heirs." Anyway, he had married her and they had had three popcorn children, one every year in a row. Miz K got a little nicer to us after the legitimate heirs came along, but that Miz Louise just turned her face away whenever we came into her view. We played with her boys afternoons, anyway, when she was taking her daily rest, and now they waved at us on the way down the aisle. Nobody had to help Miz K, though you might have thought so. *She proceeded in slow and straight, the last one in the marching line, which would make her the first one on the edge of her row.*

My baby brother, Ben, and our brother, John, and I were sitting with Mamán and Mama Emmaline, arranged in the third row of chairs from the rear by age, with John at the end on the aisle. What I shall never forget was this: the words Miz K spoke then, before she started her long walk up to the front of the parlor to take her last sight of her only son looking perfect and peaceful in his casket, before anybody moved from their seats in their own rows, Miz K spoke her first words in three days. The words came out so loud and sharp, like a clap of thunder, that no-body moved after she spoke, for what seemed like a very long time. I re-member the feeling—how hot and uneasy the air felt, and how quiet, like before the storm. What Miz K said when her voice finally came back to her at the front of that room full of flowers and mourners was fateful. Those nine words were repeated nine hundred times all around to the Pond, all over to Fort Adams, up and down the Trace, and probably all the way to Virginia. From behind that spotted black veil every single person heard it. What she said was, "Let John come up and look upon his father."

Then my brother John, the one who everybody on the Place knew our father loved the best of anybody, his firstborn son, excused himself and marched up to the front in lock step, just like the rest of the family, and did just that. He didn't lay a flower or anything. He hadn't come pre-pared for that. He just looked. The thing I can still see when I close my eyes is watching my brother John, who everybody, white and colored, had to acknowledge was the spit and image of the father who gave him his name, walk so straight with his shoulders so square in his dust-colored tweed Norfolk jacket with the belt across the back. Nobody said any-thing. That whole room full of people just sucked in their breath along with everything they wanted to say and did say later on, and they watched in the heat and the quiet. After a while, Miz Wilkie got her-self going and began to play another hymn.

When they wrote our father's obituary and all about the funeral and everything in the newspaper, not one word was written about what had happened.

That story, which is still talked about nearly a century later, is preserved only in the oral history of the Place, and it has been passed on in stories told by both races. Of course, John and my mother couldn't stay in the Small House after that. After the grieving period, everyone knew. Mamán knew it and Mama Emmaline knew it, and they started preparations for the two oldest to leave the Place. Being the baby, Ben was thought to be safe at home. People knew Mamán was getting old and needed somebody to run errands and help with things. So Ben stayed and lived out the rest of his life near the Pond. My fifteen-year-old mother was packed off to New Orleans with her cousin Irene, who was almost exactly her age. They would be nursemaids in the Garden District. They were spirited girls and looked forward to this new adventure.

My mother's brother John had been declared officially white by their father, who, we presume, had called on old friendships or paid off doctors and lawyers to get the records altered, aiming to keep his son away from the disgraceful conditions of the colored army. Since John could go anywhere he wanted, he went first to Chicago and then to Michigan to make his fortune, living as a white man but never turning his back on his family. In his old age he came back all alone to the Pond, dying of tuberculosis, and occupied for a short while a neat little wooden house near where they had been raised. I was just old enough to be taken Down Home for his funeral. Somebody set his house on fire just after he died, and all of his pictures and things were burned up.

One day a few years ago, when we were retelling this story for the thousandth time at my cousin Ben's big rambling house on the green campus of the state university where he taught, Ben leaped up and brought out this faded sepia-tone photograph of Uncle John, posed straight and smart in a tweed Norfolk jacket. And there all the stories became real.

Lightning can indeed strike twice. On a trip Down Home many years later, we learned this truth. Two old people down in the country told us the story. One was ninety-six-year-old Cousin Excel (not really family, but a part of the colored life on the Place and somebody who had known the Shepherds and the Lehmanns), and the other was ninety-three-year-old Miss Josephine, a white woman whose family had run the Pond Store after my mother had gone North and who still had every ounce of her wits about her. They both told this tale that had been whispered about behind closed doors for nearly a century. Subsequently we asked about it in several different places, and the truth was right there in the collective recollection. Everybody knew that our grandfather had been struck dead by lightning— that was enough drama to last people on the Place for a long time. But then, not a year after that fearsome event, the our grandfather's very grave was struck by lightning, and his headstone was split in two.

We were not given to discern the implications of this extraordinary occurrence, for when she told of it, Miss Josephine just looked at me sidewise and asked "Are you superstitious?" When I answered in the affirmative, she nodded and averred, "All the colored people are superstitious, aren't they?" You couldn't push her one step farther on it then. She just sighed, firmly closing the subject: "I don't think I want to talk about that any more at all." As to Cousin Ex, who was getting just a touch vague — and everybody said wasn't he entitled in his old age — he just said, "Well, it could mean one thing, and then on the other hand, it could mean something else altogether." He couldn't be moved to say anymore either. We got news just three months later that Cousin Ex had died, his stories buried right there with him on the Place.

CHAPTER 7. *New Orleans*

"*We Live in a place that is not our own.
Roses rot . . . .*"

A loose knot in a short rope,
My life keeps sliding out from under me, intact but
Diminishing,
       Its patterns becoming patternless . . .
Everything that the pencil says is erasable,
Unlike our voices, whose words are black and permanent,
Smudging our lives like coal dust,
       Unlike our memories,
Etched like a skyline against the mind,
       Unlike our irretrievable deeds . . .
The pencil spills everything, and then takes everything back.

· CHARLES WRIGHT

*The ferry to New Orleans was nearly empty, it being so early
in the morning. Irene and I were lucky we got to Fort Adams in time
enough to board, because we could hardly stand saying goodbye to Mama
Emmaline, Aunt Sarah, and Mamán. As many times as we had gone
down the river, we always knew we'd be coming back in a day or two,
and this time all of us knew it would be a while before we would see each
other again, maybe even months. They had packed us a good lunch, and
we had good strong suitcases and umbrellas, so we were ready. We also*

had the addresses of where we would be staying in this new city we were now to call home. Irene was going to distant cousins on St. Ann Street in the Quarter until she found work, and I was going directly to the people I'd be working for in the Garden District.

I had already been signed up as a live-in nursemaid for this family that had known my father. They were the Etiennes, a young couple with one little baby not a year old. After my father died, Lawyer Bramlette had talked to Mama Emmaline and seen to all the details of what my father had set out ahead of time, so it was understood before I arrived at their house on Prytania Street that I would have a room of my own and Sundays off to myself. Still, I was a bundle of nerves until I set both feet inside that house and decided that things looked okay.

Miz Etienne was the right kind, soft-talking and polite, with a nice smile, not a grinner and not a stiff-mouthed type either. Her young husband was a certain kind of man that you could call quality, one you could tell right away that treated his wife like a lady, and he talked to me with respect, too, calling me Young Miz Thelma, not Dearest or Day. They offered me a seat in the back parlor and invited me to have a glass of cool tea while we set out the details of our agreement. They let me know about exactly what they expected, and since they knew my family and thought I seemed like a right smart (meaning well brought up) young lady, they took me through the house and showed me where everything was, especially the baby's room upstairs and the little room at the end of the hall where I would stay.

That baby girl, who was named Marie-Louise, slept in the prettiest room I had ever seen, with all-white dotted swiss curtains and ruffles over the crib. Her room was twice the size of mine and had a flowered pitcher and bowl on the washstand that was much nicer than the one in my room. Well, it was a place to stay for a while, and if I didn't like it I could get some kind of job somewhere, and I could always go back home if I had to. Mama Emmaline had taken me by the shoulders and told me that over and over when I was leaving. Even though Miz Kate had been firm with her that it was time for me to flee the nest, and then Lawyer Bramlette went and fixed up this place for me, I knew I had a backup Down Home that Miz Kate had no say so over. So it seemed to me that the best thing to do was give this place a try and see if things couldn't work out.

Well, they did work out all right in one way and not in another. I didn't mind taking care of Marie-Louise. She was a nice, happy baby, and I especially liked taking her for walks every morning. I gave her her own little nickname, Lucy-Lou, and made up little songs just for her. We would walk all over the Garden District, me pushing her fancy carriage with the dotted swiss coverlet and her own little ruffled pillow. We walked over to Esplanade, up and down St. Charles, or to the river, and if the weather was fine, all the way over to Newcomb College, where the young lady students would come over and ooh and ah over Lucy-Lou. Most times they weren't sure if she was my baby or if I was her caretaker, since she had the same dark hair and hazel eyes I did. Curiosity getting the best of some of them, they would ask outright if she was mine, and I knew they were taking note that her carriage was much more expensive than my clothes. I wouldn't say much to them, just smile and walk on.

When the baby slept, I read the Times-Picayune *and drank coffee by myself in the Etiennes' garden. I loved those flowers and felt less alone out there with the roses. Sometimes I sat with Miz Etienne. She encouraged me to take evening classes at the Thomy Lafon school for coloreds twice a week, when she would put her own child to bed. The school part was all right. The high school teachers were strict in ways I wasn't used to at home, and most of the lessons were silent reading and writing so I didn't encounter any people like me who liked to speak up and have a conversation. A lot of what we learned was about wars, George Washington and Patrick Henry and such, and the Declaration of Independence. That school had maps all over the walls, though, and I really liked that.*

We learned the map of New Orleans and had to draw it, right down to the Gulf of Mexico. I drew my own map with a red line leading from New Orleans straight to Chicago. I got the idea of boarding the City of New Orleans *and getting a seat by the window and just watching all these states and cities go by. I had never been north of Natchez, and I put a circle around that. Then I would imagine what the land looked like. I had heard about the piney woods country above there. I had to guess about Tennessee, what people called the red clay country. I knew they had hills up there because that's where the hillbillies came from. We heard about Missouri, too—a lot of people from Down Home were moving to St. Louis and Kansas City, where there was music on the streets like in*

New Orleans. But Chicago was where we had some family, and I made my plan to go straight up there. Nobody we ever knew ever wanted to go to Harlem, New York, because they had too many people there already, and too many of them couldn't get jobs. Chicago, Illinois, was my hope and destination. It wasn't too far from the Mississippi River, and I put the biggest red star on my map right there, where Lake Michigan pointed straight down at the place for me: Chicago. I made up my mind to it.

In the late afternoon, after little Lucy-Lou had her nap, we would walk over to the Quarter. Miz Etienne liked for me to walk the baby twice a day, and I liked it too. This was where the excitement was. People were everywhere, and you could fill up your ears with the music, really all-day, all-night music. Men and boys playing guitars and cornets right out on the streets, and singers too. Some of the words to those songs would make you turn your head, I can tell you, and some of the boldest boys would roll their eyes and sing out "Oh, pretty woman, won't you make me a pallet on your floor."

But it was just fun. They had women singers in the clubs, too. We didn't go in those places, but you could walk by and hear them. One of the famous colored ones dressed all in red all the time. She was called Sweet Emma. They had what used to be a red-light district down there too, called Storyville, where you definitely would not want to walk. One of the cousins told us that skin color was so important in New Orleans that they had different directories for the prostitutes, organized by color! Imagine. One list of names with all-white girls, another list for light brown-skinned girls, one for dark brown, and a special directory just for octoroons. Our cousin Lemuel used to tease us to be careful so we wouldn't end up in The Book.

There were so many sides to New Orleans just about anything could happen to anybody. I could tell you about one day when I was walking Lucy-Lou around in her baby carriage and this nice-looking colored man about old enough to be my father came up and started walking right along next to me. He was well dressed and everything, with good shoes— I always notice a man's shoes—and polite, too: he tipped his hat good morning and just started up to walking in step with me. Then he asked me my name. Of course I wouldn't say my name. I looked straight ahead and said right away that I lived with a nice family and their rules were that

*I absolutely did not go out with men, so he would get the correct under-
standing from the start. After he heard my voice, he asked if I was a colored girl, and I said yes I was but I was under the protection of the family I lived with, and that they were Garden District white people. He
laughed then and said he was about to offer me a job that would put me
up in my own place and that I would make more money than I ever imagined. What I told him was that money never shined my eyes and that I
had been brought up to place value on other things. He had been watching me for a while, he said, and it was his thinking that I had a special
something about myself, and he knew a lot of nice men who would want
to take me out and show me a good time on my days off. And I could make
real money besides.*

*It began to come clear to me that what this old bald-headed man was
maybe talking about was putting me in The Book! I had to tell the man
to leave me entirely alone so I wouldn't have to get the police on him. That
stopped him. He didn't seem to be scared or anything because he just
laughed, showing that he had a gold tooth right in front of his mouth so
I would know he had money, if I hadn't yet come to that understanding.
He just tipped his hat and turned down one of the little side streets away
from the river. I wasn't frightened, just a little uneasy, but I decided to
keep what happened to myself. I definitely didn't want the Etiennes in it
at all, because the type of man Mr. Etienne was, things could get out of
hand and I might end up being sent back Down Home. I told Irene, though,
just in case that man showed up again. He never did, and after a while
she and I laughed about it. One thing I knew for sure was I would never
want even to imagine my name on any of those directories, and I learned
to be careful for the rest of the time I lived there, not to even say hello to
any man on the streets of New Orleans. That one day was enough to teach
me how easy it would be to end up in The Book.*

*But most of the time it was just fun. Irene and I used to go over to Al-
giers on Sundays, where the voodoo was. You could get your fortune told
for a dime and buy rice cakes and ice cream. New Orleans then was something different. The things that happened down there were meant to really open the eyes of young girls like us. One afternoon just at the end of
the day this man who was a regular customer in the perfume shop where
Irene worked was standing at the counter buying a fancy soap and lotion*

set from Paris, France, and all of a sudden this woman who turned out to be his wife just burst in to the store, pulled a little tiny pearl-handled gun out of her alligator pocketbook, and screamed out that she was going to kill him. We guessed he must have been buying all those sweet-smelling gifts for some different woman and the wife had found out about it.

Anyway, Irene said the wife was screaming and carrying on and waving the gun around, but she never did actually shoot it because the husband put his hands up in the air and sweet-talked her into giving the gun to him, which she did. That half-crazy woman broke down crying and the husband had to practically carry her out of the shop. After they left, the owner just put the CLOSED sign on the door, locked everything up, and then sat down on the blue silk couch in the back of the store and had a natural fit of hysterics. Irene said she herself stayed calm the whole time because she never believed the wife was really going to shoot that gun at her husband or anybody else—she could just tell, she said. Anyway, Irene ended up opening up some real expensive smelling salts and finally got the shop owner quieted down. Can you believe that woman later talked about taking the cost of the smelling salts out of Irene's pay? She didn't dock her though. I guess she probably thought better of it. It was just one of those kinds of things that happened down on Royal Street.

But there was this other thing about New Orleans that wasn't ever right. The octoroons in New Orleans had made this different little world for themselves, and I just didn't fit in at all. I understood that I was an octoroon, but that was a word that didn't mean much of anything Down Home and was hardly ever spoken. I knew people like us, my brothers and me and all the Lehmann cousins, had one-eighth black blood. Mamán used to count it out for us sometimes. She would put down the names—first, she was a mulatto herself, meaning that although she never did know her father, she knew he had been a mixed-blood man, and her mother was an African slave who had come in at Baltimore, Maryland. Then Mama Emmaline had a white father, and that made her an out-and-out Quadroon, with a little more than one-fourth African blood. Mama Emmaline wore the Montgomery name like all of her sisters and brothers, but they were true Montgomerys, and their father, Grandpapa Osborn, was a black man, so they looked different than she did.

*Nobody ever put a name to the white man who fathered Mama Em-
maline, and Grandpapa Osborn said the way things had happened wasn't
Mamán's fault, and that last girl had been gotten in his nest, so she was
his just the same as the other ones. He was a strict man, very strong and
very proper, so people didn't often challenge his word. I don't know if he
treated Mama Emmaline any different, but Mamán was very protective
of her as far back as I can remember. Then my mother Cornelia and Aunt
Sarah and Aunt Irene had a white father who was a Jewish man, so they
were nearly octoroons, and all of us were really true octoroons, since the
count didn't go any farther than that. Down Home most people didn't
care that much about all those details anyway.*

*But here I was in New Orleans, and Irene too, and we were learning
that the fine print with regard to color meant a lot more down here. Irene
herself was passing on her job. After she couldn't find any decent work
anywhere and had finally decided to apply for a job as a counter girl sell-
ing perfume on Royal Street—and got the job and a salary with it—
she just never mentioned her race and the shop owners didn't either. The
people I worked for knew all about me, of course, so I wasn't passing really, but there were so many different kinds of people on the streets in every
color you could name, Creoles in every shade too, that in some ways just
about anybody could blend in.*

*Except there was this. Somewhere in the negotiations with the Etiennes
there was some plan that I would get introduced to this little group of octoroon girls, and their idea was to find white husbands who would know
they were not really exactly white but didn't care. Those that did pass
over the line had to give up any thoughts of ever seeing their colored families again, something—you can imagine—I could never conceive of in
my mind. How would anybody know who they were without their people?
We were lucky that all of our people lived right together on the Place,
and you knew just how everybody was related to everybody else. Even
when you didn't like one person, you could always find somebody who
didn't like that same one. You all know that I didn't like Aunt Calline
much, but she was Mama Emmaline's half sister and we had to be polite
to her. I remember that she called me a womanish heifer one time too
many, and Mamán put a dead stop to her saying anything to me for a*

long while. Mamán herself used to say there was not a lot of love lost be-
tween her and Calline to begin with, and Uncle Frank, her own brother,
said Calline had just too much mouth, and not to pay her too much mind,
but we had to respect her anyway.

That's the way things are Down Home. You could find out from the
old people why there was bad blood between some families, who had run
off with somebody else's sweetheart, whose father had a bad debt—all
that. Then, too, you could always find a cousin or aunt or uncle to be on
your side when a thing didn't work out. All of the people on the Place had
known our mother, and after she died so young, most of them had kind
of a special spot in their hearts for us three motherless children. Then,
Mama Emmaline or Mamán always stood up for me, and when once in a
while even they didn't agree entirely, I knew I could always count on one
or the other of them. I cannot imagine the way people who pass over the
line just cut themselves off from everything and everybody. They have to
make up a whole new idea of who they are, coming up out of nowhere,
without anything that explains them or why they are a certain way. In
slavery days, people got cut off from their families and everything they
knew like that, and that was sad, but then there was nothing they could
do about it. But these passing people who choose to do that? I can't make
any sense out of that at all. All they get in return for giving up every-
thing is people can think they're white. People think I'm white anyway
and I don't feel any different. I have my family and my true history. That
means something.

So here I was in the middle of this thing. They called it plaçage, *a*
French name for this mixing-up of a black and white so that the black
would finally disappear. They had these big parties, and the Etiennes
would fix it for me to get dressed up and go over to Dumaine or Orleans
Street and Irene would come too and we would sit around drinking punch
with all these octoroon girls, feeling like we were being looked over like
horses for sale. Many of the Creole girls were not all that good looking,
though some were. They were different, being mixed-up with Spanish and
French and maybe even Italian along with colored, and they were Cath-
olic through and through. They all wore these little gold crosses around
their necks. Then, too, right in the middle of a conversation they would
break into talking in French and then giggle and fan themselves like

Miz K did. Well. We were used to being at the top of the pile Down Home, you know, and here we were, even with our new city bobs and our hand-worked chemises, sitting on the side! We played cards and talked to some of the young men who would come up, but it was never right. I didn't even like spraying myself with the perfume Irene would bring from the store (they gave her samples); that made me feel even more like I was fixing myself to be picked out at a market. And it was a market, all covered over with music and party dresses and fruit punch.

I hated the whole thing, and so did Irene. Neither one of us wanted to find a white husband. I did want a nice colored boyfriend to walk about with, and that was a hard thing to find. The nice colored people were mostly Creoles, and they were entirely clannish, having pretty much known each other all their lives. Then our own cousins didn't come up to snuff. So how I was supposed to meet somebody right I couldn't figure out. I started to think about leaving New Orleans and coming up to Chicago where my brother John was and some other family I liked.

After the second year I lived with the Etiennes, I went Down Home for a visit with the express purpose of talking with Mamán and Mama Emmaline and figuring out a plan to come to Chicago. So that's how I came. Irene liked New Orleans better than I did, and she had her sisters coming to visit her sometimes, but I didn't. I was basically by myself with the Etiennes and little Lucy-Lou, who were nice people all around but definitely not family. So I determined to leave for Chicago, and Irene made up her mind to come with me. As much as the people Down Home worried over us two girls coming North, and Mama Emmaline wouldn't stop crying when I left, all of us worrying about me being so far from Mamán and her and home, that was the right decision, no doubt about it. I was not sorry for one minute to say goodbye to New Orleans, and I didn't go back to visit there until after you were born. I never did try to find the Etiennes again, but once in a while after I had babies of my own and would be pushing them in their own baby carriages, I would think about that little baby Marie-Louise and that little humming song, "Lucy-Lou, Lucy-Lou," that I made up for her all those years ago, when I was just a young country girl with a head full of questions about life.

Early on when I used to try to "interview" our mother, saying who knew, I might someday write some of her stories down for the family, she would furrow her brow above her gold-rimmed glasses and ask, "Why on earth would anybody want to write a story about me? My life has been too . . . ordinary. Now who you want to write about is maybe Lena Horne or somebody like that. I read in that book you loaned me that she was born on a gambling boat or something. . . . Anyway, her people were gambling-boat people, and look where she ended up—on the silver screen!" Day was much into reading all sorts of popular magazines at the time, and her conversation was colored by that vernacular and filled with eccentric bits of information about famous people, some of which had more veracity than others. "You should think about writing about that Harlem woman who just thought up all on her own a lot of different ways to straighten Negro hair and got to be a millionaire! I read about how she came up with a Master Formula and how people all the way over to Africa use that special cream and so her daughter is getting to be a *double* millionaire. It's just too crazy to me that all the young women over here in Chicago are wearing their hair African style and the real African women over there are straightening their hair with the Master Formula. People are just never satisfied. Still, that woman and her daughter would be something to write about, if you just have to write about somebody."

Day never understood how extraordinary she was. She would not likely have described herself as courageous, but when I imagine her at the age of fifteen, leaving the only home she had ever known for a life among strangers in the peculiar metropolis that was New Orleans during World War I, I can see her squaring her shoulders and moving forward. I know she kept her loneliness to herself, for she was lonely in the midst of that hurly-burly city. I could see it on her face when she talked about that time.

New Orleans was then a city like no other. Its prolific dualities, benignly taken for granted by its citizens, shaped the radically eccentric character of the place. It was a multicultural city, but culturally segregated. Its highly stratified layers of Negro society, unparalleled anywhere else in America, were organized in large part by skin color. Uniquely, New Orleans' colored hi-erarchies were also inflected by religion, with light-skinned Ro-man Catholics at the top. The Catholic Church itself was a sur-prisingly fluid structure. The streams of visitors who found their way to services at St. Louis Cathedral could find in the church's environs not only St. Christopher medals for protection, but also St. Expedite medals, which were said to ensure that almost anything could be expedited. White inhabitants were segregated by religion and ethnicity as well, and even the wealthiest Jews, though actively integrated into the commercial life of the city, were excluded from its prominent clubs.

With no challenge to its proud title as the wealthiest city in the South, New Orleans touted the city's successful Cotton Exchange and incessant port activity. Conversely, the French Quarter was filled day and night with beggars, and colored workmen down on the levees and washerwomen roaming the streets for work earned merely a pittance. The Quarter's jazz culture gained renown and attracted hordes of tourists, and the area's free and easy prostitution flourished in tandem with re-lentless social service movements dedicated to cleaning up the city. The best areas of New Orleans were distinguished by ar-chitecturally stunning houses, and even outside the Garden Dis-trict the gardens were wildly flourishing. But ironically, the same wetness that fostered the growth of such luxuriant sub-tropical foliage was often oppressive and unhealthy. The yellow fever and malaria that had killed more than one of Day's fore-bears was still a menace, as was tuberculosis. A few years later the Mississippi River would flood, visiting on New Orleans one of the greatest national disasters in United States history and changing that city permanently, shaping its future in ways unimaginable at the time.

Our mother's first year in New Orleans lives in her memory as the wettest time of her life. It seemed to be always raining or about to, with hurricane-force winds the likes of which she had never encountered. Nonetheless, she had to see that the baby in her care was "taken out for air" whenever possible, and I imagine she didn't like being cooped up in a small room all day in any case. She read a great deal and became increasingly meditative in the solitude of her little upstairs room. Intrepid, she went out whenever she could, and although she had no real way to connect with the street life, she was entirely interested in it. And she tried to educate herself even though the school structure she encountered was at odds with her basic predilections and her country experience. Ultimately her attendance there offered little stimulation or solace.

There had been plans for Day. Both her white father and her colored grandmother had conjectured that her best option would be to become immersed in the octoroon culture that made New Orleans a haven for young people of mixed race. This hope was futile for several reasons. Practically, it would never have worked for Day because she was not Roman Catholic and she would not have embraced the trappings of the faith just for show, as some were willing to do. Socially, she lacked the urbane sophistication of many of her New Orleans peers. She was bright and had a fluent tongue, but she was still a country girl. And she was a nursemaid with no family anywhere near, except for a cousin who had no more wisdom or experience than Day herself.

It is probable that one of her main obstacles was a fundamental inability to dissemble. Octoroon culture was predicated, after all, on showing one's wares to best advantage, and this kind of conscious display was entirely foreign to her upbringing and her temperament. She wanted friends, and I am sure she especially hoped for a young man friend, but she wanted to be cared about for who she *was*, not for who she put herself out to be. It is not surprising that during those two seasons among that tightly knit community of Creole girls seeking to pass into the white world, she turned increasingly inward and began to plan for her escape to Chicago.

So I wondered what made it possible for her to stay for nearly three years, years during which she gathered a headful of stories that she would later tell her children, smiling and shaking her head at the raunchy parts. She went Down Home for irregular visits when she could and shared some lighthearted times with distant cousins. Those were touchstones for her, I am sure. But for the most part I suspect that she was sustained by her tough spirit and by an inquisitive mind that soaked up new information no matter what the circumstances. "So this is the way the world is—in this place and right now, anyway. And I'm here, so I'll give it my best try." Try she did, but gradually she began to weave her plan. Before she was out of her teens, stronger, surer, and more determined than she had been when she first left home, she found her way to the Union Station on Rampart Street and boarded the *City of New Orleans* for Chicago.

CHAPTER 8. *Day and the City*

I enter, without retreat or help from history,
the days of no day, my earth
of no earth. I re-enter

the city in which I love you.
And I never believed that the multitude of dreams
And many words were vain.

· LI-YOUNG LEE

When I first set eyes on Chicago it was everything I'd heard about. Irene and I had made the long train trip on the City of New Orleans *with no trouble at all except nerves. We were excited to the bone, looking forward and looking back all at the same time. It felt funny to go so far from Mamán and Mama Emmaline, but they had encouraged me to go. "There's more for you in Chicago," Mamán had said. "You're a young lady now. You need to be taking care of your own babies, not some other woman's. Just keep your eyes open and your dress tail down. You'll meet the right future for yourself. I know you will." Down Home people like Mamán were not much for a lot of hugging and kissing, and neither am I, but that day when I walked away from the Pond, she did hold me by the shoulders a long time, and that look she gave me was so full of love it made tears come full to the front of my eyes. Going away from home the first time, down the river to New Orleans, had been a lot easier.*

Still, the minute we stepped down off the City of New Orleans *into the city of Chicago, my heart leaped right up to meet my mouth, and I knew that I was going to like it here. I liked the way the air smelled and all the people rushing around on the platform. Everybody looked like they had somewhere to go. We did too! Uncle Jake Lehmann was coming to pick us up. He was a strange part of the family. Although he was our mother's only brother, he had been sent North by their Jewish father when he was just a little boy. His sisters never did get to know him because wherever he was, he had passed for white for a long time. After a while, though, he had married a mulatto woman and got back in touch with the family. Now Uncle Jake had gotten close with my brother John and had come with a friend to pick us up in the friend's car. We crowded ourselves in there, and we could hardly get our suitcases in, and that was exciting too. But the drive through the streets was just the best. That drive remains in my mind the all-time best drive I've ever taken, then or now. This was what they came to call by the name of Bronzeville!*

Everybody Down Home had heard about Chicago. We got to read the Chicago Defender *pretty regular, and so we got the news about how colored people were living up there. Every time somebody went up to Natchez or down to New Orleans or Baton Rouge, they would bring back copies of colored newspapers from New York City and Chicago and pass them around. Not all of the old people could read, since they had never really had a chance to go to school at all, having had to work in the fields no matter what the season was. Then, too, a lot of the not-so-old people on the Place were sharecroppers, and there was not a month in the year when something was not growing or needing to be planted or harvested. Since Mamán and Mama Emmaline could read and write, our house was the place they came to when they got ahold of a newspaper or received a special letter that needed a proper response. Nobody had any shame about it. They always brought some little thing or another to our house with them, so they could keep heads up—our shelves were full of jars of watermelon and tomato preserves, and spiced peaches and persimmon. Sometimes somebody would bring a whole pie or half a ham, and everybody in the house would sit ourselves down to a Sunday dinner whether it was Sunday or not.*

When we got a copy of the Chicago Defender *it was always entirely interesting to my brothers and me and to all of our cousins. Old people knew they were never going up North, but the young people had big ideas about going there, even if only for a visit. We read about the colored nightclubs and saw pictures of people all dressed up and stepping out of rich-looking automobiles and women wearing fur coats around their shoulders—men, too, and that part was something to look at twice. My brothers swore they would never be caught alive or dead in any woman-ish fur coat anywhere, anytime. Those papers just about made your mouth water to come to Chicago.*

Plus we had some distant family who worked on the road, as cooks or Pullman-car porters, and they really had stories to tell about all the money to be made in the big city and the nice houses people had. Now there were some eating places and nightclubs in New Orleans, of course, but the nice ones were mostly not for colored people, not to take a front seat in anyway, and in Chicago we thought nobody would have to take a back seat to anybody or go in anybody's back door. Even though, of course, some people even in Chicago were still going to insist on thinking that be-ing white was better than being colored and would try to snub you, they couldn't really make it stick, because all of the schools were open to every-body, and you could get some kind of job you could do and maintain your-self and hold your head up and raise your family.

We knew they had lowlife white and colored people in Chicago, and crime and cheating just like everywhere else. The newspapers wrote about that, too, and people who had been up there reported back on it. But our family up there were all doing really well, owning their own houses and saving money, and I was dying to go and see for myself.

We spent the week at Uncle Jake's house on Vernon Avenue, and every day we just walked up and down the streets all day long. Everything looked so different. You can't imagine. All the houses were so close together and so—citified. I'd never seen tall stone houses like those up and down Grand Boulevard, and it seemed amazing to me that colored people lived in such houses. I set my mind that someday I was going to live in Grove-land Park. It was near enough to Uncle Jake, I liked the green parkway in the middle, and the houses reminded me a little of New Orleans, but better. Everything about Chicago was definitely better in my book.

It wasn't long before Irene and I got a room together, at Leola's boarding house—she was a third cousin on the Montgomery side—and our windows looked right out on Grand Boulevard! We had two twin beds, two chests of drawers, two little nightstands, all painted white. Our room had pretty flowered wallpaper, and so did our bathroom—we were lucky we didn't have to share with anybody else in the house, the way some people did. We paid a little more, but with two of us working, it was worth it. And we were working. No more nursemaiding for me. I got a job in a factory, the Automatic Electric, doing piecework, and Irene got a job over at Alden's catalog house. Both of us were passing, but that didn't bother us. Nobody asked, anyway. And if they ever did, well, we could always get another job. There seemed to be so many places to work in Chicago. The newspaper was full of Help Wanted ads, and I read the paper every day. There was so much going on in this city that I could actually get dizzy from it. So the work was good, because there was order in it, and I could be quiet and listen to the inside of my head.

Without thinking about it, Day became a creature of the city. What she loved was all of it: the streetcars she took to and from work every day of the week, first traveling north on Cottage Grove Avenue and then, when the conductor called out 22nd Street, stepping off with the crowd and transferring west to Ashland Avenue. Mostly she was able to get a seat by the window on the second streetcar, so she could watch the smokestacks belching dark grey into the sky and the people rushing across busy streets, everybody with somewhere they had to be. She read the *Chicago Daily News* on the way home, and she felt more a part of the news every day. The bad flu epidemic had come and gone, the U. S. of A. had won the War (people Down Home would *really* have a Fourth of July parade that year), and a soldier in the U.S. Army had jumped out of an airplane high in the sky and landed perfectly safe on the ground in Ohio, wrapped up in this new thing called a parachute. She loved life in the North, and she loved Chicago. That was just the way it was. Her cousin Irene never stopped complaining about the cold, unlike anything they had *ever* known in the South, but the wind off the lake brought a flush to my mother's cheeks, and she bought a heavy, cherry-red woolen coat with buttons all the way to the chin. It was her first winter coat and she loved it too.

She was good at her job and knew it. Characteristically competent, she made extra money every week on the piecework. The conveyor belts at the Automatic Electric Company were fast-moving, calling for the kind of quick dexterity that was natural to her—she was, after all, a country girl, young and strong, with high spirits and a tremendous sense of optimism. But there was this: there were no visibly colored girls on the line. No one asked her any questions about race, and she didn't volunteer any information about herself. Many of the girls didn't speak English anyway—in the company of raw new immigrants from Poland, Lithuania, and Italy, her close-mouthed way went without much notice. This was the kind of tacit passing that allowed my mother to gain a foothold in Chicago in 1918 and 1919.

And then all of a sudden that first long winter came to an end, and with no spring intervening, the fabled Chicago wind died down to a hot breath on the cheek, and a heat as dense and heavy as any she had known Down Home descended on the city. The streetcars were steamy even with the windows open, and their lacquered wicker seats scratched her skin through her thin summer cotton dresses. Day was settling in. She understood heat, and although people seemed a bit testier or slightly more sullen at the end of the afternoon, she washed her hands, combed her bobbed hair, and boarded the homebound streetcar pretty much as she had learned to do.

That day she would not forget was July 27, 1919, one week to the day after her twentieth birthday. It was too hot, that was part of it. The temperature had been steadily in the high nineties for over a week. For those who weren't acclimated, the antidote was to jump in the lake and cool down. She lived only a ten-minute walk from the 31st Street beach, but she basically didn't like to be there. Although Day loved to *look* at the lake, there were just too many people hanging about, she said. Too many people gathered in one spot made her uneasy.

That day by the time the streetcar got halfway across 22nd Street, the cross streets were filling up with all these people. Police cars were coming from all directions, what seemed to be hundreds of people were yelling and pushing, and it seemed for a minute like something absolutely crazy was going on. The motorman just sped through without stopping—he wouldn't even let anybody out at their regular stop. We were really trapped inside the streetcar, without understanding any of what was happening, and you can believe we were all scared to death, thinking maybe the War to End All Wars might be starting up all over again, and this time it would be right here in Chicago. The streetcars finally opened the doors at the end of the line, all of them spitting out onto the streets what seemed to be the whole entire South Side, all of it in a wild race to get out.

When I tried to push through the crowd toward home, I had to work my way through what felt like a sea of screaming and cursing colored men. The white people had all stayed inside the streetcar, which had just turned itself backwards and sped back the other way. The noise was the most deafening sound I had ever heard. People were smashing windows, fire engines with sirens screaming driving straight into the crowds, and all I could think of was What is happening? What is happening? After running, pushing like the rest of the crowd, and nearly having the breath crushed out of me, I finally got home.

Then Day found out what was happening. One young colored boy fleeing the heat had floated out too far into the lake on a raft he had proudly made himself. He had drifted from the safety of his own beach, across an invisible line, and into the waters off the shore near 29th Street, which everybody understood to be restricted to whites. He had been caught in the water by a gang of white teenage boys and stoned without mercy until he could no longer keep his balance, and he had finally slipped into the water and drowned.

When news of this reached the adjoining colored neighborhoods, people, enraged, stormed the 29th Street beach and beat up anybody white who happened to be hanging around. Word of the incidents spread through the whole South Side, and it turned out that what Day had gotten caught in the middle of really *was* the inception of a war, a race war, the great Chicago race riots of 1919. Thirty-eight people were killed, and more than five hundred people, both black and white, were wounded. Those who didn't want to fight stayed inside their houses. Some guns were shot out through open windows, like on New Year's Eve. These were rural people, after all, only recently hunters of raccoons and opossums, and they had brought their shotguns with them to Chicago.

My mother didn't report to work for a day, but after that she braved it. The mayor had finally called up the National Guard, and it really did seem like a war. The streetcars had started back to running, but everybody was tense, and the motorman told my mother she was crazy to be riding through colored neighborhoods and asked what she was doing there anyway. She just said she was going to work. Years later I asked her if she hadn't been really scared, and she said that she was a little, at work especially, because she had to listen to a lot of bad talk there against the coloreds and not open her mouth. But she was saving money and sending a little something Down Home every two weeks. She needed the job. The uneasy feelings stayed around until the weather got cold again.

When she talked about it years later, my mother said it had been a bad summer all around, especially for people who lived on the South Side. About a year after the riots, it came out in the papers that a big baseball scandal that had been happening at that same time had ended up with nearly half of old Mr. Comiskey's cheating team being banned from the game for the rest of their lives. She couldn't take it in. This was the city of Chicago, and Lake Michigan didn't—and couldn't—belong to any one race just because they decided to say it was theirs. There was enough water and enough beach for a thousand little boys to play and swim, colored boys right along with white. And baseball players already made more money than most people even though they only worked half the year, so why did they have to sell out their team and the whole city just to get their hands on a little more money? To my mother all of this mess seemed calculated to keep her reminded that, North or South, people couldn't ever just leave well enough alone.

CHAPTER 9. *The Ring*

Life has knocked over the lamps
and rearranged the maps.

· AUGUST WILSON

This was to be her day of reckoning. It had to come sometime, after all. She just didn't know when or how.

"What is *this?*" That was my aunt Irene asking. She never minced her words, just came right out with what was on her mind. "What, now, *is* this?" With those words, my mother said, the whole story just had to come out. It was probably time, anyway. She had been putting on her white cotton nightgown, and Irene had gotten a glimpse of the slender platinum circle that she had been wearing on a chain under her clothes for nearly three months by then. "What is *this?*" is what she repeated, insisting on an answer right that moment.

My mother wasn't one to avoid a thing, either. Not when it came to that point. So she told. She told Irene, with whom she had shared the neat room with its two narrow, white, chenille-covered beds nearly every day since the *City of New Orleans* had opened its doors and let them and their suitcases out at the smoky 12th Street station. And she begged Irene not to tell anyone else. She wanted to tell her brother John first, and then Uncle Jake and Aunt Mable. Then she would write Down Home and explain everything. Then she and her brother John together would tell Dr. Cullom, the man she was supposed to marry at Christmastime, just four months away.

The thing Day told was this: she had been married to that handsome John Rone from Shreveport for all of these three months. They had gone over to Englewood and gotten married secretly on June 9, his twenty-fourth birthday, in a brief, formal ceremony performed by a minister someone had recommended, before witnesses, strangers whose faces and histories were unknown to them. Day had brought home a flower-bordered wedding certificate with all of the signatures to prove it. She brought it up now from the bottom of her middle-sized suitcase, the one with the tricky lock. She slowly unwrapped the newspaper from the parcel to reveal the certificate, official in its unbelievable gilded frame, naked to the world, confirming the tale she was telling now in a hushed, uneven voice.

When I was a child and my mother would tell the story of their marriage, she would take that marriage certificate out of her lingerie drawer and read it aloud, the names, the witnesses, and tell us about the strangeness of being there without any of her family. It was not the way she had imagined things. The date, June 9, 1924. All in an elegant, old-fashioned script. It was, to her and to us, a sacred object. My mother had fallen fatally and fatefully in love with the man with whom she was to create a family and a life.

She had been engaged to another man for some months when she met him. Her brother John and her Uncle Jake had set that whole thing up, assuring her future. Albert Cullom was a dentist who occupied one of the nicest houses on Vernon Avenue, a block on which he owned several other buildings. He was a serious, light brown-skinned man with freckles, short but possessed of a certain assurance, with gold-rimmed eyeglasses that made him look what my father would later call Important with a capital I. My mother and the dentist had been introduced, and as she was a prize and he was approved, after a brief formal courtship they were engaged. My mother said they had never kissed.

She liked the stained-glass windows in his house, but she just didn't like him in *that* way. He didn't laugh enough and he was definitely too short. She had a good job, and her intention from the beginning had been to be a bachelor girl. Every time she thought about what her life would be like beginning at the new year of 1925, she would feel as though someone had put a blanket over her head and she was being smothered.

And then she had met John Rone. Her family knew him and liked his older brother Fred, who had lived around the corner from Uncle Jake. Fred was a tall, prepossessing man, somewhat stern, with a friendly wife and two well-mannered little girls. His baby brother, John Drayton, called Dray, had come up from Shreveport out of the blue, and as the new boy from Down Home, he had been introduced to everybody by Leola, my mother's landlady and distant cousin. My mother said that the first time she saw him, she thought he was just entirely too good looking, and that could mean trouble. He was tall like his brother, but not stern at all. He had an immaculate look to him, and she liked that. He had an easy, laughing way with the men and a nice, polite, well-spoken style of talking with the women, to old Leola as well as to the younger women. If he had been a little less good looking, she said, he might have been just right.

Well, her cousin Irene thought he was just perfect. And unlike my mother, she wasn't engaged yet, so she flashed her laughing blue eyes at this country boy who seemed like he'd been in the city all his life. That posed a bit of a problem for everybody because Dray had made up his mind at the very party where they met that my mother was The One for him, and in his book, engaged did *not* mean married. They kept running into each other. Everyone had parties all the time, and everybody played Whist and sometimes Blackjack—that was mostly a men's game, but some of the women played from time to time. The drinking was mostly a men's thing too. Fred Rone's wife, Sarah, joined the men as easily as if she were one of them. But not Day. She had something unusual about herself, something that set her apart. She was beautiful, that was certain. But she had something else—a look in the eye, a certain independent spirit. She seemed not quite standoffish, because she was friendly enough, but somehow unavailable. It was definitely not the engaged part, though. He could see in a minute that the dentist was no match for that one. Her sassy cousin Irene was fun, but Day was a major challenge. He made up his mind.

I have never known the details of how they managed to come together. It would not have been easy. Her brother John didn't trust Dray Rone farther than he could throw a stud horse. This younger Rone was not at all like his brother Fred, who was much admired as a strong, solid man, a person of property. This Dray, a singer of songs, was too careful of his looks and his car and got along far too well with women. Did John Shepherd see the growing attraction between his sheltered sister and this audacious newcomer? Likely, a good deal of their courtship was carried on during the day—I imagine these two star-crossed young people skipped a few days of work.

My mother fell madly and irretrievably in love, and as she was brought up the way she was, the only thing to do was give in to my father's imprecations to marry him immediately. Engagement be damned, family be damned—life was full of promise and they should grab their star. So she did it, but she made him pledge that he would wait for her to come to his bed until she could find the right moment to tell her family. That moment eluded them for three months—there was always some reason not to disturb the peace. And so he became increasingly impatient, and I imagine that under pressure Day got careless and undressed to put on her nightgown in front of Irene, whose quick and canny glance discovered the wedding ring on a chain around her neck.

All hell broke loose. Irene left immediately to tell my mother's brother John, who was so heartbroken at such unbelievable news that he wouldn't—couldn't—speak to my mother for eight days. Uncle Jake was simply furious at the betrayal. Irene, in an angry tirade, insisted that my mother move out immediately, saying she couldn't sleep another night in the same room with such a person. My poor mother, who had to move in then with her husband of three months, wept unstoppably for days. For the rest of her life she said that on that fateful night she had wished to join her own dead mother on the other side. As an adult I mused over how Day's precipitate decision to marry for love echoed her father's headstrong choice on behalf of his colored family. Surely this resonance was unconscious, but after all, her father was a Shepherd, and so was she.

When I was a child, the family talked about the secret marriage with great emotion. My father had the easiest time with it—after all, he had won. He always said our mother just couldn't resist his ability to sing love songs. My mother's brother John went to his grave with serious reservations about my father, and he occasionally tried to get her to leave him. Her Uncle Jake was permanently cold to my father, although he welcomed my mother and her children into his home. My Aunt Irene soon married another man, a very solid citizen who prospered well beyond Dray Rone, and she and my mother made up and went back to being best friends for the rest of their lives. Still, these were deep-country river people with long memories, and silt from the anger never disappeared. Three years after my mother's funeral, my sister Audrey and I went to Aunt Irene's ninetieth birthday party, given by her daughter Arlene, who had grown up with us. When I leaned over to congratulate my aunt Irene with a kiss, she spat out these words with surprising energy and spite: "Your mother just *had* to have her that pretty man." My father had been dead for over twenty-five years, my mother for half a decade.

I imagine how the Louisiana sheikh—that's what my mother called him—must have wooed the already spoken-for Day Shepherd. His intuition about people was uncanny, and guessing accurately that she had been brought up with the crisp freshness of white cotton underthings, he would have introduced her to a self she hadn't known with flesh-colored silken lingerie edged with thick cream-colored lace. She would have blushed, pronouncing him extravagant and more than a little bold, but she would have worn the fine chemises or slips anyway, surprised by their softness. She would have dressed and undressed in the cramped bathroom she and Irene shared, hiding the underthings in the bureau under her neatly folded pajamas.

My father wooed my mother unceasingly until the end of his life. When I was a child, he would come home on Sweetheart's Day, Valentine's Day, or some anniversary understood only by the two of them and present her with a slender, beribboned box, which she would open carefully, smoothing the tissue and exclaiming over the beautiful nightgown inside but chiding him for spending money foolishly. You are one pound-foolish man, she would say. I didn't understand, then, the erotic nature of such gestures, but I knew that although my mother shook her head at him, she was pleased. Then there was perfume—White Shoulders was what he brought to her, a discreet scent fitting for that interior ladylike quality of her. A bottle of it stood on her bureau throughout her life, though she used it only on rare occasions. There were chocolates too. I heard my aunt Irene speak of the extravagance of his chocolates, saying my mother should have known right off that Dray Rone would never accumulate anything. More than half the time when our Father stepped off the streetcar on payday, he had a box of Bunte chocolate cherries under his arm. We never got it straight whether the chocolate was meant to keep her happy even though the money was so meager, or whether it was simply evidence of his lifetime love affair with her.

As to the other characters in the drama, there is this frequently retold story: A few days after the news of their marriage had been made public to the entire Louisiana-immigrant South Side through one of those amazing word-of-mouth telegraph systems that sustain communities, my mother was walking down 35th Street by the Louis Theater. She ran into the ill-fated Dr. Cullom, who had his dental office on that street. He said with some dignity, "Miss Shepherd, I understand that you have married Mr. Rone." She answered with her head held high, "You have that accurate." He said, "I think then that you should return to me the gold wristwatch which I gave to you in commemoration of our former engagement." She said, "You have that accurate," then snatched it off her wrist, thrust it at him, and walked away. My mother told this story with laughter. She just never could see herself married to that man (probably in part because of her rebellious side), though she did like the woman he later married, and after some years the two families took up a somewhat distant friendship. He was never our dentist, though. That would not have worked out at all, so we went to a different one on 30th and Prairie.

Decades later Dr. Cullom, a widower by then, came to our father's funeral, and after a respectable time he became a rather frequent visitor, chasing away Day's loneliness with laughter about the old days. He brought her chocolates too.

CHAPTER 10. *A Stern Destiny: Chicago Found and Lost*

> What will the scribe recall, who tells of the stern destiny of all these women forever condemned to pregnancies, who, in order to foresee the day's weather and figure out what labors to take on, are expert at deciphering the prophecies of the wind?
>
> · HECTOR BIANCIOTTI

Once I read an article titled "Chicago: Lost and Found." For my mother, the decades of the 1920s and 1930s could have been captured in the title "Chicago: Found and Lost." She had found an easy sense of fit, of habitation. She had learned the city's byways, conquered its intricate network of buses and streetcars, identified the neighborhood shops with the best produce, and found a butcher she could trust. She had saved money before she married my father and continued to afterward. For each of the months she worked at Automatic Electric, she tucked a few paper-clipped one-dollar bills and a folded five into an envelope and placed the envelope in what she called, and would call throughout her life, the Book. A dark-blue-covered edition of somebody's almanac, the Book resided in her lingerie drawer, and it was her homely version of a safe deposit box. After we grew up, she always kept about a hundred dollars in small bills in the envelopes so that any of her children could have access to "mad money" when and if we needed it. One or another of us intermittently did.

In early 1926, "big pregnant" with their first child, Day quit her job, and she would not resume working until World War II. As was customary, Day went Down Home to deliver her baby, boarding the *City of New Orleans* once again with her cousin Irene, fortuitously pregnant with her own first child and due close to the same time. These two cousins, nearly exactly the same age and as close as sisters, did most things in symmetry. Their husbands had little in common and little affection for one another, but that didn't seem to interfere with the women. Men occupied a different world anyway, one of evenings and Saturday afternoons. The women shopped together on weekday mornings and visited on Sundays. Especially after the children were born, they spent innumerable hours together walking their babies. My mother and my aunt Irene sat in Woodland or Groveland Park, or when the weather was fine, on the lakefront. They talked endlessly.

From my own childhood, after they had had four children each and my mother had added one more, I remember their rich, irrepressible laughter floating on the air. Being Southern ladies, though, they covered their mouths when they laughed, as they had been taught. From the beginning, these two had so much in common they were nearly twinned. A couple of weeks after my sister Zoe, named Zoreda after a favorite sister of my father's but always called Zoe, emerged at nearly nine pounds, my aunt Irene's baby son, named Weathers after his father but always called Sonny, was born. My mother's Aunt Sarah, my great-grandmother Emmaline, and the same midwife, Miz Elnora from down by the Pond, attended both births. (Somewhat surprisingly, our grandfather's old friend and family physician, Dr. Brandon, came to look in on my mother's delivery.) Both babies were brown-skinned and dark-haired. They looked enough alike as to be sister and brother.

In the Deep South, this color thing had implications: Aunt Irene, unacknowledged and unsanctioned daughter of an Irish friend of my grandfather, had very fair, freckled skin, fiery red hair, and snapping blue eyes. With Day's creamy skin and hazel eyes, the two girls were mostly taken for white and not subjected to the daily harshness of Jim Crow. With brown babies in their arms, things changed on both sides of the color line. My brown-skinned oldest sister was a child of amazing beauty, with gleaming black hair and eyes, a small straight nose, and a shapely mouth. She attracted so much attention both down South and back in the city that my mother was worried that vanity would take hold and ruin her. But the colored people said right out that it was a good thing that child was so particularly pretty, prettier even than her mother, since her coloring was not fair and this might otherwise have worked against her. White people stared, some boldly and some covertly, but mostly said nothing. Still, both women now had to confront the long waits and inferior facilities that daily insulted colored people below the Mason-Dixon Line. Explicit coloredness in public arenas, on trains and buses, in shops, and at toilet facilities, was now their challenge. Laughing at the ridiculousness of a world that could, and did, change on you in a minute, the two absorbed these new constraints with flat acceptance and a sashaying walk. They sat with indestructible dignity on segregated benches, each with a beautiful brown baby on her hip. Within a few months, Aunt Truelove Lehmann added her own brown beauty, a girl.

As things turned out, the birth of her first child marked a new period for Day, the end of her working-girl years and the finding of her true vocation: mothering. Day was astonished by her passion for the child. She had once proudly designed herself as a bachelor girl, and even after marrying Dray Rone and loving him as she did, she carried within herself a defined, pristine independence, something that belonged only to her, a legacy from her mother. That contained, coherent inner spirit broke open when her body opened to loose this first child both into the world and into an inner sanctuary she had not expected to share.

The severing of the umbilical cord was a necessary physiological phenomenon, but the tie between herself and this daughter was astonishing, primordial, *irreversible*. It was not mystical or even fanciful, but *basic*, and she understood for the first time why women in primary cultures bury umbilical cords, an ancient act that affirms their relationship to nature, to history, to time. What came to her was the most powerful, most sure knowledge of her life: it was a knowledge made of memory, of what had been lost to her, and in some inchoate way it came to inhabit the empty space where her mother had been. Being a mother was just exactly this complete intimacy with another being, this overwhelming oneness. The child belonged to her as no one ever had, and she would love this child without reserve and without caution. What she had known mutely as irremediable loss, the premature death of her own mother, was now called forth as a gift, to be hers until the end of her own life over half a century later: the Bachelor Girl became a Mother.

My parents lived then in the upper-floor apartment of my uncle Fred Rone's red brick house on 32nd Street and Vernon Avenue, just a few steps around the corner from Uncle Jake and Aunt Mable's graystone house where my mother had lived her first weeks in Chicago. After Zoe was born, they determined that the time had come for their family to move, perhaps now to Groveland Park, where the beautiful center greensward and the rows of solid-looking family houses with wrought-iron fences and stair balustrades recapitulated in a Northern way what she had liked about the Garden District in New Orleans. It was a blow to her that they couldn't possibly afford a Groveland Park place, but she would walk those secluded streets often, and for years she maintained her dream of living in a house there.

Ultimately the young Rone family occupied the first floor of a small house on nearby Bowen Avenue, having moved there in time for the birth of their new baby son in early 1929. There was never any question that he would be named after his father, consonant with Southern tradition, but their first son, John Drayton Rone Jr., had his own permanent nickname, Jay. Without a drop of Spanish or Creole blood in him, Jay always had something of the delicate, refined look of the Spanish aristocrat, and as their prized boy, he brought a new kind of light to his parents' life. He had pale brown skin and large, limpid brown eyes, and he didn't resemble anyone but himself.

Jay was a somewhat delicate, croupy infant, and his arrival as the first Rone born in Chicago had been marked by a long labor, a difficult birth, and extended postnatal visits from a public health nurse. The stories were repeated so often that I can almost see the small bedroom with its corner washstand, the efficient nurse with her navy blue uniform and her black bag full of thermometers, suction implements, plasters for my mother's back, and bandages for the baby's navel, which just wouldn't heal. In those days mothers stayed in bed for fourteen days after their babies were born, and in some cases considerably longer. They called it being in confinement, or lying-in. The nurse made my mother drink strong tea for her woman's ailments and gave her something to make her breast milk extra rich to strengthen the baby. She prepared breakfast for Zoe and bathed and dressed her too. She washed what had to be hand-laundered, changed the sheets for my father to take out to be laundered, and scoured whatever needed scouring. In early 1929 all of these mercies were available at little or no cost, and for many of the amazing women who served in these ways, such work was a blessed calling.

Over that long summer both Jay and my mother regained their strength, and the small Bowen Avenue house was filled with light and children's patter and the flowering plants that grew prodigiously with Day's careful nurturance.

In the cold winter of 1929, my father was laid off from his job at Armstrong Paint Company. That's how they talked about it—laid off. No severance pay then. Just a pink slip and the bitter shock of having no work. And suddenly there was no work to be found anywhere. The relentless impact of the Great Depression on their young lives cannot be overestimated. The thriving South Side neighborhood they had come to call their own was emotionally and spiritually devastated. The black-owned Binga Bank, in which the young Rones had been slowly building a modest stake in a future that seemed assured, turned away unbelieving customers and barred its entrances. Once-vibrant commercial strips like those on 31st, 35th, and 43rd were lined with boarded-up storefront windows and padlocked doors.

And even the burial insurance companies wobbled, creating pervasive anxiety within the colored community. A fine and seemly burial was, after all, one of the anticipated rewards of life in Chicago. Notwithstanding all of the lately romanticized literature of the outsize New Orleans funeral with its carriage parades and jazz bands, a significant portion of Chicago's colored middle class had little patience with such unrestrained extravagance. What my parents and their friends wanted was the dignity of a substantial coffin; impressive flowers from family, friends, clubs, and associations; a good, not-too-long eulogy by a minister who did justice to the English language; a few songs people could sing, led by a really good singer who did not "shout"; someone to read Lord Byron's "Crossing The Bar"; and a repast following the funeral with food and drink in egregious quantities. All of this cost money, and people had made regular weekly payments to ensure that their last rituals would not pose any family hardship. In 1929 and 1930 many previously comfortable colored families had to settle for much simpler end-of-life commemorations. Still, relatives and friends contributed what they could to maintain traditions and pay proper respect.

Family stories of the Great Depression were always told to us as lessons, the cautionary tales of those who had survived. Of course, colored doctors and lawyers were the most obvious survivors—the professional classes maintained a small but steady supply of cash no matter how much that supply was diminished from the heights of earlier times. It is for these reasons, in large part, that people like my father wanted their sons to study medicine or law, as first and second choices, and encouraged their daughters to marry professional men. I only knew one *girl* from my high school who became a medical doctor; she later went on to become president of Spelman College. We never knew a woman lawyer, although there were some about, particularly in the political realm. Decades later, when my own oldest daughter informed us upon her graduation from Yale College of her plan to go to law school, my mother was momentarily speechless. She subsequently accepted this radical decision but admonished her granddaughter to please not become manly. Day did not live long enough to see our youngest daughter, Lynn, become a criminal defense attorney. This would have called for a great deal of explanation indeed.

Although our father was a factory worker, many of his friends were professionals. He lacked the necessary formal education, but it is for other reasons that it seems unlikely he would have succeeded in those endeavors. Always somewhat improvident, Dray Rone was, I think, what might today be called a certain kind of intellectual, a highly individualistic and self-directed seeker of information. He read incessantly, borrowing an amazing spectrum of books from anywhere he could get them, scouring all kinds of magazines and his friends' medical and law journals, reading assiduously three or four newspapers a day and weeklies like the *Chicago Defender* and *Reader's Digest*, and engaging anybody with sense in endless argumentative conversations about world events. And I do mean world—our family's idea of community extended from our block to Washington, D.C., from the Panama Canal to Versailles. His maternal grandmother had been a full-blooded Choctaw Indian, so our father had accrued an unusual store of knowledge about the Bureau of Indian Affairs and the Trail of Tears. Something of a hypochondriac, he was very interested in traditional Native American herbal healing and was in frequent conversation with our local pharmacist about arcane remedies.

And that's only for starters. Dray was inordinately eclectic in his interests and pursuits, impulsive and improvident with his time and money, and much too restless to hew to the heavy hours of study required by higher education. It was Day's frugality and thorough attention to structure that would keep their heads above water, but without his income, even the best-laid plans went awry. One can only imagine this man's frustration and despair at the falling apart of the life he and his young wife were in the process of building.

They were two ambitious young people, country-raised to look life straight in the eye and, perhaps more important as a shaping factor, both left motherless before the age of eight. These two had both emerged from lives resembling the Chinese I Ching: hardly anything was stable for more than a little while, everything was perpetually evolving into something else, mothers died on you long before you were ready, and fathers died too, leaving you with little but the wind behind your back. They had both gone as far South as the Mississippi River would carry you, one on a ferry boat and one on a freight train, seeking to somehow locate a way that made sense. New Orleans was a way station, and Day Shepherd had known almost before she got there that it was too small for her. True, the legendary open diversity of the town was there, but for a young woman with her dreams—to find real work, to hone her skills, to create a home—she had to go North.

Dray Rone, more flexible and less starchy than the young woman he married, might have stayed in Louisiana, but as he told it, when he was seventeen years old, a cross-eyed white gal started following him around and turned up just once too often. If he had taken her up on her idea, he could have been lynched. Then again, if he hadn't taken her up on it, she might have taken a mind to accuse him of something, and he could have been lynched anyway. The South was full of such stories, and the Scottsboro Boys case a few years later became an example of why he had done the right thing by hopping a train to Chicago to join his older brother Fred and his sister Ola. His upstart older sister Bessie had gone halfway and decided en route that a city the size of St. Louis was a better place for her to make her mark. And make a mark she did, developing a significant reputation as a volunteer with the St. Louis NAACP while managing a white-collar job at the segregated Homer G. Phillips Hospital and turning her elegant home into a sort of refined boarding house for young colored interns and residents.

All of that generation of Rones were each in their way exceptional people. Their father had been born in slavery, son and "carriage boy" of a South Carolina plantation owner and an African house servant. The story is that when freedom came he was fifteen years old; he ran away with the best carriage and never stopped running those horses until he got way up in East Texas. After a little time there, working occasionally as an unofficial land-grant surveyor, for he had learned to read and write and was said to be exceptionally proficient with numbers, he had found a tall half-African, half-Choctaw Indian wife named Eliza Roberts and moved on to northern Louisiana.

I've no idea why they settled up near Shreveport, but there Dray's father started a one-room school for newly liberated slaves, determined that they too should learn to read and write and count. The small church that used to house that school was still there in the 1940s, when I was a child, and a handmade sign saying "John Rone, Head Teacher" was still there, too, along with two trellises flanking the door, one blooming with red flowers and one with white. John Rone had dropped the slave name Drayton along the way and had invented a new identity for himself. He was a radical, I think, because he named his older sons after abolitionists—my Uncle Fred was Frederick Douglass Rone, for example. The reason he finally gave the hated slave name of his actual father to his youngest son, the last of fourteen children, is lost in the mists of history. I've always wished we knew.

My Aunt Ola recollected around her lace-covered dining room table in Chicago how "Papa used to make us dust off the benches between the classes. Not just children, but men and women came in during the day and during the evening, and many of them came in direct from the cotton fields, with cotton dust all over them." We have a photo of their father, a smallish man, sitting stiff and proper in a Victorian suit and tie while his tall, half-Choctaw wife stands, buttoned tightly into her heavy long dress, with her hand on his shoulder. One terrible year when my father was just seven years old, his parents followed each other into the grave only months apart. People down there said his mother died of a broken heart; she simply couldn't live without the man who had shaped her life for so long. But there was also this: tuberculosis. In the first decades of the twentieth century, tuberculosis swept through those parts of the South like a mad river, and when too many in one house died, people would burn the house to the ground. There was yet no real knowledge of germ theory, and this seemed—and probably was—the best thing to do.

My father, the sheltered baby of the family and orphaned at seven years old, was shuttled about from one older sister or brother to another. Some were kind and generous, some resented having to take care of him. As soon as he grew up enough, he tried to join up with the army. A few weeks after he was inducted, they found out that he was actually just fourteen years old, and they forced him out unceremoniously. He was tall, six feet three, and smart and a great talker, so he landed jobs wherever he went—Texarkana, Arkansas; New Orleans; Joplin, Missouri; and finally Chicago, where he arrived when he was nineteen. A man who had already tried out a number of things, he quickly got a job at the Armstrong Paint Company and met and married our mother, whom he liked to call "the best of the bunch." By the time they had two babies and a little money in the bank, things seemed, for perhaps the first time in his life, pretty well set up.

And then came the Depression. In my own mind I think of it biblically as the Fall. When my father lost his job, it was a deep shock to him—and to her—that he couldn't find other work, any work, anywhere. This is how she told it:

All those days and weeks and then months of his going out mornings and coming back empty-handed. Cold and dark when he left out, and cold and dark when he came back home. We just had to let go of about every dollar we had left, and nothing came in—nothing at all. Aunt Mable brought us bags of groceries, my brother John would come around when we weren't expecting him and bring an envelope full of cash. He didn't want me to let your father know, but I had to tell him and set a little aside after buying food—a grown man is entitled to have some money in his pocket. Your father started cutting hair—yes, barbering—in the house, for those friends of his who could afford it. That lined his pockets a little, and some of them would bring staples in a brown bag when they came and leave the bag on the table when they left. I felt shame. The worst part was when Sarah, Fred's wife, would come trailing Ernest Douglass's little wagon and carry up food for us. I just hated her to see that we had fallen so low. Fred never did lose his job—the people at Armstrong kept him on, and somehow it felt a little disgraceful that your father hadn't made a place like that for himself, especially being a nicer person by far than his brother ever was.

Anyway, we didn't have any choice about these things. We had the children, and even though Uncle Jake and Aunt Mable invited us over to dinner pretty often, and so did Fred and Sarah, we had to stretch things at home for our family. John Rone hated to go to my family's house anyway—Uncle Jake never got over blaming your father for taking me away from Albert Cullom, and now he could congratulate himself on that judgment because Cullom was a dentist and a landlord, after all, and had a permanent good living. So some of the time I went over to my family with the children and John Rone went off with his friends, and they would eat dinner at somebody's house or another. Your father insisted that we invite those men to our house for dinner too once in a while, and I would cook up big pots of turnip greens and cornbread and stretch a little piece of salt pork a long way for flavor, and we always had crates of pecans and black walnuts and cane sugar sent from Down Home, so I could put together something sweet with that. It was a time, and we just lived it day by day.

After a while and a lot of thinking about what in the world to do, some of these men cooked up this partnership to make bathtub gin— moonshine—and sell that. You can guess the market for alcohol never did go out of favor, and when they changed the laws so men couldn't buy anything to drink in a legal establishment, well, men were just going to find a way to make it the way they used to. Your father's friends, the Evans brothers, were from Henning, Tennessee, that same town where that Alex Haley, the man who wrote the book Roots, grew up. They had been country boys, and they knew everything you needed to know about grain *alcohol. It was their idea to set up the still in the basement of our house and, of course, they would pay off our landlord to shut his eyes to it. It was their idea that your father could work out a deal with the police for protection. They would pay part of the profits for that, but your father should be the one to set the whole thing up, specifically because Dray Rone could charm the birds out of the trees, and he got along well with those Irish policemen, always laughing and talking, and they gave little treats to our children when I walked with them down Oakwood Boulevard.*

Well, they worked it out, and they started the business, and—they made money. This was the whole thing—things changed too fast. After all that time of just toughing it out and being ashamed in front of your family and feeling like you had to take low when you knew people like Uncle Jake and my brother John were thinking, "Didn't I tell you?" . . . after too long and too much of worrying if you'd be able to feed your own little children, well, when the money started to come in fast and the liquor was in the house and the men were coming and going, your father started in to drinking with them. I hated to see them at my door, you can believe it. They would sit around and drink and talk too loud, and I hated for my two little children to be anywhere around them, so I'd go walking or go visit with Irene. Then in the little private time we had, your father and I would argue.

So things got bad between us, and he would go out and spend good money on a new bedspread, or on some fancy nightgown for me to make up for it. Sometimes he would give me a fat envelope of money to send Down Home—Mama Emmaline, Mamán, and Lil Auntie weren't having it too easy either. Once after a bad argument where I really put my foot down and said I would just bar my door and he could stay down with the men and drink himself to death, he got Sarah to go downtown with him and help him pick me out a sealskin coat. I liked the coat, but I never got over being sorry for his involving Sarah. She stayed tight-lipped about that coat to the day she died, even though Rone had helped Fred out with money more than once during that time. It was bad, but it wasn't all bad.

The all-time worst thing: One time this something happened that was really scary, but funny at the same time, and, in a way, lucky for us. About a year after this incident Roosevelt would be changing the law again, and people would start back to buying their liquor in the stores where there was a lot more choice than the strong white lightning bottled on Bowen Avenue. But even though Prohibition wasn't over yet, you could feel the change coming. The men laughed and said Al Capone was going to have to find a new business, and so was Dray Rone. I think your father had gotten tired of it anyway; it felt a little dangerous because strange people were coming into the house all the time, and some of the policemen you had to deal with were hotheads too.

It was this police incident that finally made up your father's mind to close that business. He had worked out a deal with the regular police who patrolled our neighborhood—I didn't know the details and I didn't want to, believe me. If any of those blue suits looked sidewise at me on the street, my heart would start pumping. They knew. They knew who I was and what illegal business my husband, my children's father, was involved in. They knew we had strange men coming in and out of that house, some of them being suspicious characters. And money was passed. I continued to hold my head high, although sometimes I used to wish I could disappear because of my respectability being put on the line, and I couldn't even walk the streets in my own neighborhood and not have to hit that fact in the face every day.

This one day the whole thing cracked open. Somehow a new team of blue suits had been assigned to our little area, and we didn't know them and they didn't know us. Needless to say, they hadn't been a part of the profit-sharing, and when they nosed out that something was going on, probably because of all the comings and goings and the nice cars on the street, they got a couple of paddy wagons together and rolled right up to our front porch. Our lookout—there was always a lookout—telegraphed the danger somehow to the men in the basement, and they grabbed the still and put it in our big steamer trunk. Your father grabbed me and sat me down hard on top of the trunk, and put Zoe in one arm and Jay in another. By then, I was big pregnant with a third baby, and so when the police burst in there we all were looking like a Madonna picture in a Catholic church, sitting on the trunk with the fringed shawl from New Orleans on top of it, with the still hidden inside, nice as you please.

The policemen just stared hard at us and shook their heads as though they couldn't believe it—we figured they might have thought I was some kind of pitiful woman caught up in white slavery with a bad set of slick,

colored hoodlums. Whatever. They didn't say one word, just asked the men
to come outside and answer a few questions. Your father, always well-
mannered, excused himself, kissed his children, and left with his hat in his
hand. When he came back home, he told the story that it had been a little
worrisome but everything had come out okay. I never knew if any money
changed hands or not. They had complimented him on his pretty children,
he said, told him to take care of his pregnant wife and to stay out of
trouble and away from bad company.

Now, as she said, not long after that my father got a job working in a factory right on the streetcar lines. Our mother was so
relieved to have her house to herself again she said she spent
nearly the whole of that first winter inside her own four walls
with no one but her babies. She cleaned her house with even
more fervor than usual, scrubbing and polishing every visible
and invisible surface, every pot and pan, every glass in every
picture frame, dusting under every bed. She cooked with renewed joy and pride, seating her husband like a king at the head
of the table, presenting again the rich meals she had lost any interest in preparing because she couldn't stand those moonshine
men "stuffing themselves all hours of the day" in her kitchen,
over which, for that time, she had lost all jurisdiction.

The centers of hegemony that colored women like my mother
enjoyed in their homes had no counterpart in the lives of men
like my father or most of his friends. When the men did have
jobs, they were menial, and the men were reliant on the hard-
won and even harder-sustained good will of white supervisors.
Most colored men who were not professionals worked under un-
remitting pressure at unrewarding tasks and were always careful to keep as low a profile as possible. When they said, as my father often did, that their home was their castle, they meant it.
It was the work of women to create a home that was respite and
release for their men. Men's work had one purpose: to ensure a
paycheck for the family.

So when I think about my father, I wonder if it might have
felt strange for him after all that time on his own to have to keep
regular hours again, to be accountable to someone else. Did he

miss the camaraderie of all those Southern colored men, and their stories and their laughter? Did he miss the drinking, and the heady sense of power that sometimes accompanies that? He was young, after all, and soon a whole new world would be opening up. FDR was changing everything, it seemed, and there was yet another baby in the house. My brother Arthur was born late in the spring of 1932, a fat, round, gold-colored baby with a head full of golden brown curls and huge, thickly lashed, gold-colored eyes. We used to laugh that he was a born entrepreneur. A charmer like his father with his mother's pragmatism and grit added, he was destined to do well in his many childhood business ventures, and after he became a soldier, he was a man's man who could drink anybody alive under the table. Making fun, people said ruefully that the liquor-business years had marked his daddy's second boy in the womb.

My father, John Drayton Rone Sr., also known as Dray. Wedding por-trait. The "Louisiana sheik" is in full regalia, looking young and vulnerable even with his elegant camel-hair coat and hat.

My parents' marriage certificate, June 9, 1924. Some months after Day's death, we found this tattered document, folded and torn at the edges, among her insurance and Social Security papers. We had it restored to its original splendor for posterity.

Dray Rone with his and Day's first child, Zoe, 1926. There is no maternal counterpart for this portrait of our father with their firstborn. It is likely that Day returned from Down Home, where she had given birth, and presented their daughter to her husband for the photograph.

*My great-grandfather Berthold Lehmann and his twin brother Karl,
ca. 1873–1874. This photo pictures two dashing young German immigrants
amid the accoutrements of their prospering life as merchants to the river
trade. We do not know which brother is which.*

My uncle John Shepherd in Natchez, ca. 1903–1904. This elegant photograph, taken near the time of John and Day's mother's death, was damaged by fire and stored away in my cousin Ben Lehmann's basement for many years. For our family it is an important visual image representing the care and decorum that characterized the Shepherd children's upbringing.

Uncle John in St. Joseph, Michigan, ca. 1915–1918. An interesting portrait depicting Uncle John as a sensitive but determined young bachelor. Passing for white at the time, he purchased land in Michigan and in outlying areas of Chicago, carefully invested monies left to him by his father, and built a tidy sum to be shared with his siblings.

My sister Zoe with Daddy's car, ca. 1935–1936. She strikes a saucy pose in her Sunday best in front of Daddy's prized automobile, a tangible benefit of money from the moonshine years. Her Shirley Temple curls, public evidence of the quality of Day's attentive mothering, were finger-molded with a wet hairbrush, a lengthy and painstaking process.

I won the annual Beautiful Baby contest and the privilege of riding on a float in the 1938 Bud Billiken Parade. The criterion for winning was neither beauty nor charm, but the number of tickets sold for the contestant. Our father's sister Ola Walker's formidable energies and ticket-selling skills ensured my victory.

Zoe with her husband, Pat, at the Club De Lisa, ca. 1947. This famed nightclub, located in Bronzeville, drew an interracial patronage from all over Chicago. With top entertainers, a BYOB policy, and no cover charge, the Club De Lisa was a glamorous and popular tourist destination. After closing then enjoying a brief renaissance, the club saw its ultimate demise in the 1960s.

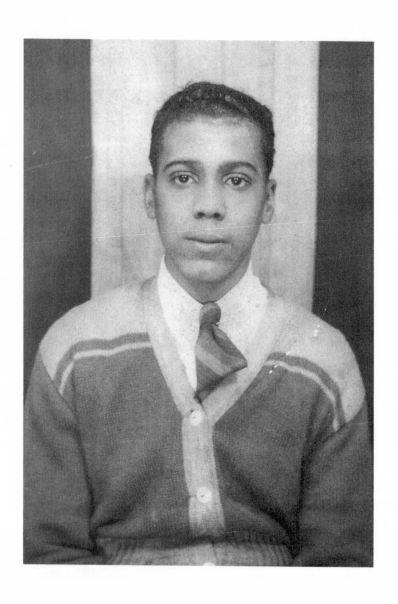

My brother Jay in his Phillips High School sweater, 1944. Always serious and careful about anything he put his mind to, fifteen-year-old Jay wore a white shirt, ironed by Day, and a tie, tied by his father, to high school every day.

My brother Arthur, still in the U.S. Army, 1953. Tanned, handsome, and jubilant because the siege of Okinawa is behind him, Arthur displays a young man's eagerness to rejoin the civilian world. Day loved this picture and kept it permanently displayed in a frame on her dresser.

Audrey and me at Christmastime, 1947. Always intensely sisterly, we loved posing together each Easter and Christmas, resplendent in our curls and our Margaret O'Brien hats from "the Hub," Lytton's Department Store downtown on State Street.

Day and me at my graduation from the University of Chicago, 1955. Day was so delighted to watch one of her own march out of Rockefeller Chapel with degree in hand. The white gloves and hats that we both wore were testament to the esteem in which we held the occasion.

Day at the wedding of her baby daughter, Audrey, with a family friend, August 1970. Day is wearing the designer pink silk dress we talked her into purchasing for the wedding. She had never in her life spent so much money on a dress for herself, and she never would again.

*Day, once again in her extravagant pink silk dress, this time at the
wedding of her first granddaughter in 1984. She had tied a pink silk scarf
around her neck to disguise her relentless weight loss. It was the last time
she wore the dress, which was put away in a garment bag until her funeral
two years later.*

My mother with me in the garden she loved, late summer 1985. This is one of the last photographs taken of Day. Increasingly frail in the last months before she died, she didn't like the way she looked in this beautiful picture taken by a family friend. She worried that she looked much too thin.

A Shepherd/Rone clan gathering, spring 2000. Day would have loved to have been with what she called "all her generations" at our daughter Lynn's joyous wedding in Lakeside, Michigan. Nearly every person in the family was there, and some of Day's great-grandbabies resemble her profoundly.

My great-aunt Sarah Lehmann's gravestone. On a research trip Down Home in 2001, we found the colored cemetery on the Place. We were unable to find our grandmother Cornelia's gravestone, but we did find this one marked with her sister's name. Aunt Sarah occupied the small house next door to the one the Shepherd children were raised in.

A Lehmann cousin and friend walking down a path on the Place.
On this memorable journey, cousins led us on a walk for miles down the
overgrown dirt roads of the Place. We had known there were 5,000 acres,
but we were surprised and quieted by the sheer vastness and dense green of
the old estate, so visibly and sadly abandoned.

A small house on the Place today similar to the one my grandfather Arthur Shepherd built in 1895 for my grandmother Cornelia and their children. We came upon this empty, neglected house in a far corner of the Place. A local cousin told us that it likely bore some resemblance to the original Small Houses inhabited by our forebears.

The Pond Store as it is today. It was fascinating to visit the still extant store, now a landmark with a Web site on the Internet but largely unchanged since our mother's childhood. The present owners told us vivid stories of the turn-of-the-century times when our mother's grandfather and his twin brother were important merchants in that area.

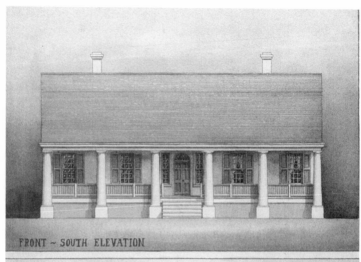

FRONT ~ SOUTH ELEVATION

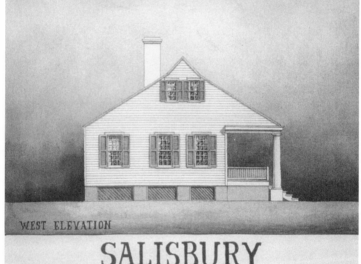

WEST ELEVATION

SALISBURY

An artist's rendering of the Big House at Salisbury, ca. 1898. Courtesy of the Louisiana State Museum, Baton Rouge. The museum owns this early image of the house as it appeared before the turn-of-the-century construction of an additional wing. Most of the original furnishings, paintings, and other objects from Salisbury's drawing room were given to the museum, where they are still on view in the decorative arts galleries.

CHAPTER 11. *The Post-Depression Years*

The city was the sanctuary of the word,
of the gesture and the geste, of struggle.

· EDOUARD GLISSANT

My mother told only a few stories of the years between 1932 and World War II. What I know is that the emergence of Franklin Delano Roosevelt exceeded in importance any historical or social phenomenon ever talked about in our family, including Babe Ruth and Halley's Comet. The exception would be Joe Louis. Joe was special, intimate, *ours*. We called him the Brown Bomber, and when he won, we all did. The cheering around a thousand radios was inflected with the symbolic assurance that the entire *race* was strong and brave and would fight to the death to win. When Joe lost, everybody even *close* to being colored grieved.

FDR was the first American president since Abraham Lincoln who meant anything to colored Americans. He promised an end to the joblessness that had sapped the body and spirit not only of individuals, but of the black community as a whole. The strength of local power in fledgling social and economic institutions had been decimated, and the idealistic promise of a prosperous future had given way to despair. FDR gave back to colored people a sense of possibility, restoring that hope that had engendered the Great Migrations from the South to places like

Chicago. It cannot be emphasized enough that the early FDR years had an unprecedented significance in the black psyche not simply because of his commitment to putting the country back to work, as important as that was, but also because the vivid message to people of color was about the restoration of dignity.

Eleanor Roosevelt partnered with her husband in communicating and promulgating a new insistence on *dignity* for people of color, and that was medicine for ailing souls. When Mrs. Roosevelt confronted the Daughters of the American Revolution over their refusal to allow the great African-American contralto Marian Anderson to sing in Washington's Constitution Hall and invited her to sing instead on the historic steps of the Lincoln Memorial, that gesture was celebrated throughout the colored world as the magnificent act it was. Langston Hughes wrote, "I hope [God] drives the Jim Crowers out of their high places, [and] smites White folks down, . . . [but] I hope He lets Mrs. Roosevelt alone." This was a new kind of leadership for these United States, and especially for its colored citizens. My father worked then for the WPA (what they called FDR's WPA) at a job that, while lacking in status, brought with it the dignity of daily work and a reliable weekly paycheck. The moonshine business had come to a halt, and both of my parents devoted their time and energy to the rearing of their growing family.

There was a rich ferment among colored people nationally during those years, and Chicago was the nexus for much of it. For families like ours, the single most important organ of communication was the *Chicago Defender*, a weekly founded at the turn of the century and edited by Robert S. Abbott, who was understood to be our own. Like almost everybody else, he was a Southerner who had migrated to Chicago. The *Defender* had a vast national circulation, distributing more than forty thousand papers a week in Chicago colored communities alone. And it was not just read—it was liberally quoted at every gathering of family or friends. It attracted the best of colored writers, and thus were we educated by people like Langston Hughes, who had a regular column called "Simple Says," much beloved by my father and his friends. Its subject was usually an ironically humorous tale of the plight of some colored citizen that ended with the subsequent delight of clever redress. The excerpt below is from one characteristic column, titled "Simple on Military Integration." It is of particular interest in light of changes that occurred over the half-century after it was penned.

"Now the way I understand it," said Simple one Monday evening, when the bar was nearly empty and the juke box silent, "it's been written down a long time ago that all men are borned equal and everybody is entitled to life and liberty while pursuing happiness. It's in the Constitution, also Declaration of Independence, so I do not see why it has to be resolved all over again."

"Who is resolving it all over?" I asked.

"Some white church convention—I read in the papers where they have resolved all that over and the Golden Rule, too, also that Negroes should be treated right. It looks like to me white folks better stop resolving and get *doing*. They have resolved enough. *Resolving ain't solving*."

"You can't blame anybody for history," I said.

"No," said Simple, "but you can blame folks if they don't do something about history. . . . To be shot down is bad for the body, but to be Jim Crowed is worse for the spirit. Besides, speaking of war, in the next war I want to see Negroes pinning medals on white men. . . . I have not yet seen a picture in *no* papers of a *colored* officer pinning a medal on a white soldier. I'll bet there isn't a white soldier living who ever got a medal from a colored officer. I want to see colored generals commanding white soldiers."

"You may want to see it, but how can you see it when it just does not take place?"

"In the next war it must and should take place," said Simple, "because if these white folks are gonna have another war, they better give us some generals. I know if I was in the army, I would like to command white troops. In fact, I would like to be in charge of a regiment from Mississippi."

"Are you sober?" I asked.

"I haven't had but one drink today."

"Then why on earth would you want to be in charge of a white regiment from Mississippi?"

"I can see myself now in World War III," said Simple, "leading my Mississippi troops into action. I would do like all the other generals do, and stand way back on a hill some-wheres and look through my spyglasses and say, 'Charge on! Mens, charge on!' Then I would watch them Dixiecrat boys go—like true sons of the old South, mowing down the enemy.

"When my young white lieutenants from Vicksburg jeeped back to Headquarters to deliver their reports in per-son to me, they would say, 'General Captain, sir, we have taken two more enemy positions.'

"I would say, 'Mens, return to your companies—and tell 'em to *charge on!*' Next day, when I caught up to 'em, I would pin medals on their chests for bravery. Then I would have my picture taken in front of all my fine white troops—*me*—the first black American general to pin medals on white soldiers from Mississippi. It would be in every paper in the world— the great news event of World War III. . . . It would really be news! You see what I mean by *solving*—not just resolving. I will've done solved."

Hughes's column reflects in microcosm what the *Defender* was: a newspaper by, for, and about *colored people* with all of the pitfalls and triumphs in their lives. It was said that Mr. Abbott never liked the term *colored*, or the term *Negro* either, preferring to use the word *Race* with a capital *R*. He was what was called at the time a Race man, joining the followers of W. E. B. Du Bois, whom some of our father's friends called Gray Uncle Wee Bee and whose NAACP journal *The Crisis* was published in New York for the black literati. People also read Charles Johnson's high-culture journal *Opportunity*, produced for the national Urban League. We had a Chicago branch of the Urban League near 35th Street, and our father and some of his friends went there frequently, using it as a current-events library. Race men were our respected scholars and pundits, those upon whom most colored people relied for clear, informal, and *reliable* analysis of the national and local news and its present and potential impact on their lives. No one expected this from the white newspapers, which people also read, of course, although those papers' perspectives always had to be absorbed and weighed alongside those of the *Defender*.

Within his own circles our father constructed himself as a Race man. He was certainly not politically powerful, but he was a great talker with a keen interest in and analytic insight into the local and national cultural context and its implications for the lives of colored people. There was, in that decade, a major shift going on in the political power of black Chicagoans, and men like my father were vitally interested in local politics. Blacks were actually being elected to the U.S. Congress and taking on significant roles here at home in City Hall. One of our community's most admired business leaders, Oscar DePriest, tall and commanding and so fair-skinned as to appear white, was known to be entirely dedicated to the advancement of the race. He had been elected as U.S. congressman from my parents' South Side neighborhood in 1929, the year everything fell apart. He was unseated briefly by one Arthur Mitchell, a graduate of Booker T. Washington's Tuskegee Institute, but it was Mr. DePriest's later successor, the flamboyant and vastly powerful Bill Dawson, whose name and power loomed over Chicago's colored communities in the 1930s and who remained a tremendously potent figure throughout our childhood.

In the 1940s Big Bill Dawson lived a few blocks from us in a looming red-brick mansion secluded by an imposing black iron fence. We children used to hang out outside the house hoping for a glance of this man who everybody said could fix anything, get your son into the state university, get your daughter a job in a city licensing department, or unlock your grandmother's old age pension checks when they were tied up in the bureaucracy. "Big Bill D" occupied a uniquely legendary status both before and after his death, epitomizing Black Power prior to the invention of that nomenclature, and that power was making itself felt in the city's workforce in visible ways. Men and women of color were gaining footholds in the railroad and packing house workers' unions, and the AFL and CIO enrolled thousands of colored workers. According to the studies of St. Clair Drake and Horace Cayton, blacks constituted more than a third of all Chicago labor union members in 1937. Chicago was justifiably acknowledged for its central role in these political changes, but also for the distinct aura of glamour that surrounded its colored leadership. People loved to talk about the strength and manliness of Big Bill D, who, although in relentless pain much of his life following a train accident that resulted in an amputation, never let on that beneath his exquisitely tailored pants was an artificial leg.

Chicago's thriving policy racket, with its high-living policy kings, added its own aura of glamour and danger to the daily challenges in the city's depressed communities. One important partnership was led by the celebrated Jones brothers, one of whom was assaulted on the steps of City Hall and, it was widely reported, relieved of some $50,000 in cash. Whether exaggerated or not, that was a prodigious sum of money to be carrying on one's person in 1928, and the abrupt and permanent disappearance of the flamboyant brothers from the city lent weight to the story. Some said that they emigrated to their villa in Mexico for a while, but as the legend goes they ended up in southern California, where they prospered in the real-estate business. Certainly the stories, however apocryphal, of icons of possibility such as these, at whatever levels of colored society, provided some relief from the pervasive despair of the Great Depression and its aftermath.

Things did not turn around quickly for people like my parents even as the Depression began to recede. There was still job and housing discrimination and ineradicable poverty. New migrants continued to come up from the South, including several distant cousins of ours, and many found it hard to get a foothold. Others were sustained by FDR's federal relief programs. Still, for the young John Rones, the FDR years were relatively comfortable, and by the time I was born in 1936 they had moved to a larger first-floor apartment at 40th and Vincennes Avenue.

My entry into the family was welcomed with special enthusiasm by ten-year-old Zoe, who was desperate for a baby sister. There would have been *two* sisters for Zoe, but my tiny twin sister did not survive the difficult delivery. My mother always thought that an X ray in her seventh month had negatively affected her, since precautions later employed were not in place in those days and the doctors had whisked their ill-fated baby girl away before my mother ever set eyes upon her.

The particularity of my having been born as the surviving twin was for years quietly erased from the family history, and even my birth certificate lists me speciously as a single birth. When in my second pregnancy I began to gain weight and girth at an incredible rate, both my mother and Zoe brought up the possibility of a twin birth, retrieving the long-suppressed stories of my own nerve-racking though triumphant arrival into the world as a twin. My doctors, impatient with questions that to them reflected old wives tales, insisted that there was absolutely no evidence of twins. There was no perceptible double heartbeat, nothing palpable to suggest the presence of two fetuses. In 1960, after all, when breeding women were still thought within medical circles to be slightly hysterical, women like me accepted medical assessments as the product of the superior technical knowledge and experience of their doctors. Against my mother's admonitions I put the idea of twins out of my mind until our beautiful twin girls, Lisa and Karen, were born within five minutes of one another, both blessedly healthy. My husband and I were astonished. The family women were entirely vindicated.

By 1939, when my mother's last child arrived, John Rone had moved his family into the apartment where they would live for the longest period of their life together. It was the site of my growing-up years, the place where my mother's spirit resides most richly in my memory. It was nearly contiguous to Michael Reese Hospital, where my baby sister, Audrey, was born. She was brought home from the hospital wrapped in a pink blanket fragrant of hospital baby powder and placed in my arms to hold—my very first memory. The apartment was on the top floor of the tallest building on Calumet Avenue below 31st Street. The back of the building faced west to South Parkway, a tree-lined street whose name was later changed to Dr. Martin Luther King Jr. Drive. Originally called Grand Boulevard, this was the same street that had so enchanted Day when she had taken her first magical ride through Chicago's South Side.

The transition from the eponymous Grand Boulevard to a careworn lower South Parkway was a visible metaphor for the situation of colored Chicagoans. Not only had the long decade of the Great Depression exhausted idealistic hopes for the South Side, but the new realities of a changing community were making themselves felt wherever colored people lived. Although many of the newcomers in the second wave of the Great Migration settled on the Near West Side of the city, newly immigrating families also crowded into cut-up apartments on the South Side, where shrewd, unscrupulous landlords quickly created the kind of tenement kitchenettes evoked in Gwendolyn Brooks's poems, in collections like *A Street in Bronzeville*.

KITCHENETTE BUILDING

We are things of dry hours and the involuntary plan,
Grayed in, and gray. "Dream" makes a giddy sound, not
    strong
Like "rent," "feeding a wife," "satisfying a man."

But could a dream send up through onion fumes
Its white and violet, fight with fried potatoes
And yesterday's garbage ripening in the hall,
Flutter, or sing an aria down these rooms

These new Chicagoans, many of them former sharecroppers, were often less educated and less skilled than their earlier counterparts, and they had a significantly more difficult time gaining a foothold in the city. There were still solid bourgeois houses and apartment buildings lining South Parkway, but they were gradually interspersed with more marginal dwellings and transient businesses, and ultimately the Ida B. Wells public housing complex. These working-class dwellings were named for the celebrated black activist who had died during the Great Depression and whose daughter Alfreda Wells Duster lived with her five children just a few blocks away. I visited Mrs. Duster's two youngest children, but she and I had our own friendship. Her gentle, strong voice and measured advice meted out around her dining table were significant in shaping my thinking about the world and my possibilities in it.

This early example of Chicago public housing bore little relation to today's tragically deteriorated structures, now being demolished in favor of new ones closely resembling the original Ida B. Wells homes. Ubiquitous flower boxes adorned the low-rise apartments and small private dwellings situated around a central community building, Madden Park, where young people enjoyed swimming or ice skating in season while their mothers, fathers, and grandparents saved to accrue down payments on their first homes.

South Parkway had changed to accommodate a changing colored populace, but the community still provided a remarkably stable, safe, and largely wholesome family environment. Day's younger children grew and thrived there, playing outdoors on the central green parkway, which was bordered by thick hedges that accommodated our games of hide-and-seek, but were removed, sadly, in the more tumultuous 1960s, in an effort to deter crime.

Our apartment was only a ten-minute walk to Groveland Park, the other place that had taken ahold of Day's imagination, and she would almost always walk in that direction when she was planning to sit out and let us children play. Holding my hand and pushing Audrey's baby buggy, she would walk down South Parkway, passing the impressive stone structure of Olivet Baptist Church. Our Aunt Ola Walker lived across the street from that famous church and had become a member there. She and another of my father's sisters, Bessie, the St. Louis one, were joiners. It is said with some accuracy that I take after them, because our mother was decidedly *not* a joiner, although she could be a great talker within an intimate group.

We would then walk east, to the Stephen A. Douglas monument, and Day would tell us stories, reminding us how lucky we were that that puffed-up little man had lost the presidential election to the near-sainted Abraham Lincoln. If the weather was fine, we would walk across the 31st Street bridge to the lakefront. She liked it that we could see just a little piece of the lake from the window of her bright kitchen kingdom. Most things of importance were talked over by that window looking out at the lake. Although my mother never really liked beach environments, within her composed, practical exterior lived a woman of incredibly rich texture, and I suspect that Lake Michigan's far horizon, like the green New Orleans resonance of Woodland Park, allowed her access to some dreaming place in herself. This may be fanciful though, because certainly she never spoke of such things.

What Day did speak about was the family, us and the cousins, and the wide world around us and what was happening in it, always personalized. Some of her talk was from newspapers and the radio. She read, not voraciously like my father, but regularly, whenever she could make space between her overwhelming homemaking responsibilities; her visits with Aunt Irene, Uncle Jake, and Aunt Mable; and her less frequent but still more or less regular Sunday afternoon visits with other cousins. She especially loved her youngest cousin, Willie Edward, who lived a block or two from us on Prairie Avenue with his warm and funny wife, whom we only knew as Sugarbabe, and their four children.

There's a somewhat characteristic family story about Sugarbabe, which happened on the occasion of her funeral in the 1980s. Our mother told it this way:

Sugarbabe was one of the kindest women I ever knew. She was not a pretty woman, but short, round, and very dark-skinned, and people wondered more than once how she got a good-looking, blue-eyed man like Willie Edward Lehmann. He laughed about the curiosity and said to let them wonder until the sun went down, Sugarbabe was his secret business. When Sugarbabe died I was really sorrowful for little Willie—he got old so quick after that. Even though their children were all grown up, he grieved hard and never did really get back to himself. He did see to it that she had a nice big funeral with a lot of flowers.

It was a shame you couldn't be there, dahr-ling. It seems as though you are always traveling somewhere or another! You've just got the hot foot, like your father and his people, but we made sure the ribbon on our flowers said "Aunt Dearest's children," so you were in it one way or the other. And at least you were represented by your husband and daughter, who went to more than a little trouble to get there. You know that they went first to the wrong funeral home? Your poor husband thought he knew how to go, since he had gone with you to so many family funerals over the years, so he didn't even bother to get a specific address or anything. He and Claire just showed up at Leak's on Cottage Grove, and when they didn't see one single face they could recognize at all, things got confusing all around. The thing was, the only name they knew was Sugarbabe. Now you know that name wasn't on the service list, and wouldn't be listed even if they had been in the right place, which they were not. So believe me, they didn't know what to do and were just going to have to go back home, when some one of the mourners saw these two entirely confused people and just went up and asked may I help you.

Well, it's a bad thing that Chicago is so segregated, I grant you that, but the good part of it is that colored people all know the whys, whats, and wherefores of just how things go, and anybody at Leak's that evening could just about guess that if you were looking for the services of somebody named Sugarbabe, and Leak's was where your family usually went, there would be a pretty good chance that this Sugarbabe person might be in repose at only one or two other places. The first place they suggested was Rayner's, a few blocks north, and with directions Bob and Claire drove right over there, and the first person they saw was your cousin Leroy Ransom, so they were relieved to no end. Once inside, of course, they learned from the obituary that Sugarbabe's real name was Helen Givens Lehmann, my cousin Willie having been the baby of that branch of the Lehmann second generation, those who grew up in the other Small House, sharing a yard with us. This lets you know that people need to know each other's real names.

A major part of our lives revolved around the family. It is said that colored people all over the world will ask each other upon first meeting "Who are your people?" My mother's people were her brothers and her cousins, Shepherds and Lehmanns. Her brother John had moved to St. Joe, over in Michigan, with his wife and their only daughter Myrtle. They were tacitly passing, and Myrtle was a beautiful dress model for the garment industry. Thin as a whippet and chain-smoking Camel cigarettes, she used to come and visit us from time to time. Somewhat estranged from her own mother, Myrtle adored her Aunt Dearest whom, like her father before her, she called Day, and my mother loved her dearly. Myrtle would sit at our dining room table and she would smoke a mile a minute and push her shining hair behind her ear, and she and Zoe and my mother would laugh and laugh. This lovely young cousin died a mysterious death before she was thirty years old, breaking my mother's heart. People said it was fortunate that her father had preceded her in death, because he could not have survived that loss. Myrtle's death, relived for months and even years, belonged to the family.

Day's story about Myrtle has sifted through the generations:

Your sister Zoe, always given to anything mysterious or superstitious, never stopped insisting that after Myrtle died, she came back into our family in the person of your first baby daughter, Claire. Zoe told this crazy story to all of you younger children, and it is a story that just won't go away. You'll probably be telling it to your own girls. I take it with more than one grain of salt, myself, but I think I'm only one person, and I'm not the hoodoo kind, myself.

Anyway, the way Zoe always told it was this: Myrtle's spirit used to come and sit at the foot of Zoe's bed. It wasn't scary or anything—it just seemed perfectly natural, and in a way even comforting. After Claire was born, there were no more Myrtle visits—ever again. That was the final end of the ghostly visitations. Now, I have to admit that Claire really does have a more-than-passing resemblance to Myrtle, and that is a little strange. You know Claire pushes her hair behind her ears all the time, exactly like her long-dead cousin she never once laid eyes on. Myrtle was a constant nail-biter, too, and so is Claire. The main difference is Myrtle smoked a mile a minute, and I know Claire has never smoked.

Although my daughter has never really accepted the family's mystical claim on her as Myrtle reincarnated, she still takes it all lightly, recognizing it, in her lawyerly way, as a moot question. Myrtle's death constituted the formal end of that branch of the Shepherd clan. I always thought my mother loved Myrtle so especially because she was the only fruit from the branch of her oldest brother John, one of the most mythic figures in our tribal tale. He was, as old people used to say, Day's Lord and Jesus Christ. She worshipped him. Only five years older than she, he had served as an intimate father figure all of her remembered life. Although her actual father had been a responsible man, and had taken over some aspects of her training, it was her brother John (always spoken of with that fraternal prefix, to distinguish him from any other John, our father or our cousin John Lehmann) who could always make her laugh until tears came to her eyes, and it was he who was her real teacher and shaper, her tender disciplinarian and wise counselor. She told us this story:

I was in the garden one day when I was about eleven or twelve years old, pulling up turnips and mustard greens for dinner. It was my week— each of us children took a turn, one week at a time, and we had to plan, prepare, and serve the main meal and clean up afterwards too. I had been doing this since I was a very little girl, I guess almost since the death of my mother.

Anyway, that was what I was doing, and suddenly I felt a little light-headed, and leaning down, I noticed a trickle of blood running down my leg. I ran to the house to investigate myself and learn what I had done to start up that bleeding—it was like I had cut myself somehow, down in my private places, and hadn't felt the hurt. I pulled out our round zinc tub and filled it with cold water and took off all my clothes and got in, with a towel around my shoulders. I don't know how long I sat in that tub of water, but I remember I was starting to get cold and shiver a little, when my brother John came into the house and found me sitting there with my knees up and that blood on the water.

"Girl, get up out of that tub and put your clothes on," he said. "What's wrong with you?"

I said I thought I'd cut myself on some thorny root.

"Didn't Mama Emmaline tell you anything?" he said.

"Tell me what?" I asked.

So it was my brother John who explained to me about women and the monthlies and told me I would have to be double sure now to tell him if any boys were after me because it was dangerous for girls to be too close around with boys after the monthlies made their presence known. I didn't worry about boys in the first place. I liked to run with them, and they let me because I could do everything they could do and ride horses faster than they could but I didn't brag about it. My brother John made me to know that I'd better not be riding any horses while I was bleeding down my legs because I could damage myself real bad.

He left me alone, then, saying that he would tell Mama Emmaline to explain to me all about how girls with the monthlies kept themselves clean and all that. That part embarrassed him, I could tell. You'd have thought that being a farm girl I would've known all these things, but I didn't know any of it, and after Mama Emmaline came home and we had a talk, she made me promise not to tell Irene or any of Aunt Sarah's girls about what had happened to me. "They'll learn in their own time," she said, "and this is your private business." I still don't like to talk about this kind of personal information, but I told my own three girls the whole story when each one got to be ten years old. I decided it was better you all should know beforehand.

My sister Zoe told me that every time she set eyes on Uncle John after hearing about the blood on the water, she was embarrassed. I was too little to be *in* that, but I heard the story retold many times in my life, way after Uncle John died.

There was little love lost between Uncle John and my father, though they had come to a kind of grudging peace, both knowing but not talking about the history. Uncle John had, after all, rejected my father as an inappropriate suitor for his sister, having a more solid option in mind. After our parents had children, Uncle John came to visit us with some frequency, and it was always an occasion for high spirits in the house. He would stay two or three days, regaling my mother all afternoon with stories of Down Home people, and she would cook the most sumptuous meals, even making special desserts like peach and blackberry dumplings.

When the men would sit down together after dinner, they would talk of how the Depression was finally letting up and how great FDR was and how nobody in his right mind would trust Tom Dewey with that little shit-eating mustache of his. They would drink bourbon, though more sparsely than was usual with male visitors to the Rone house, and afterwards, when it was time for us to go to bed, Uncle John would gather us all around him in the boys' brass bed and tell Down South ghost stories. The scariest one was my mother's favorite, about these three huge dogs, one of whom had one eye smack in the middle of his forehead. I always have had a vivid imagination, so I would cringe under the covers, and my brothers would torment me for days, chanting that spooky choric line "Dang-dang—Sanko—ride, ride away."

Sometimes Uncle John and my mother would take us with them to visit Uncle Jake and Aunt Mable while my father was at work. We never went to visit Uncle John's house though, understanding that in those days when he was living in St. Joe, Michigan, he was passing. His wife, Aunt Ethel, knew all about us, but she seriously disliked my mother, and that was mutual.

When Uncle John was diagnosed with the TB, as they called it then, our mother, who almost never cried, wept for days. He went back Down Home to live then , and Day took her oldest children with her to help set him up in his small house on the Place. Of course he went back to die, and we felt it, although no one talked about it. He went without Aunt Ethel, whose name was forever after a stone in my mother's mouth. He was taken care of by family: Lil Auntie was still alive, and their brother Ben was there, and they nursed him and sent for my mother when he passed. On that trip home she took her all her children with her, and one of my earliest memories is of the absolute white blankness of my mother's face on the train on the way back, and of how quiet our house was for the longest time. That second great loss of her life was more deeply felt, I think, even than the loss of her mother, and it had permanent resonance.

Our mother's younger brother, Ben, the one who stayed Down Home, married a sweet-natured, proper-talking school teacher down there named Rose, and they had four children, who were very close to us. We used to exchange visits with them every summer—a few weeks down there for us, a few weeks up here for them. They were all boys except for their pretty sister named for our grandmother Cornelia and called Connie. My uncle Ben prospered on what used to be the Place, becoming a contractor after REA (FDR's Rural Electrification Administration) came out there, building small houses with shining new kitchens that sold out even before they were finished.

During the war Uncle Ben moved to Chicago for a time, staying with us and working for a year or two as a foreman at the Link-Belt factory not too far from our house, passing for white. This Uncle Ben, with hard blue eyes, was more than a little gruff. More of a disciplinarian than either of our parents, he used to scare us a little, but when the grown-ups gathered after dinner to roast peanuts and tell stories, he was just such a good imitator, what they called a gamemaker, like the rest of the family. After the war was over, he went back Down Home for good and built a big, modern house for his family, replacing the one we used to stay in as very small children. This new house was large and light and always fragrant of sun-bleached linens and the homemade preserves simmering on the huge black wood-burning stove—Aunt Rose never would have an electric stove because she just couldn't trust them. But that foreign-seeming stove with its flaming heart was one of the primary reasons—

among many—why I looked ahead with anxiety to our trips Down Home.

Every summer when we were taken on these trips Down Home, riding the *City of New Orleans* to McComb, Mississippi, we were met by relatives then taken by bus on to Woodville, then out to the Pond, near the Louisiana border. These trips presented us with the ingrained challenges of Jim Crow: All of the colored people had to change cars at the Mason-Dixon Line in Cairo, Illinois. There were the water fountains and bathrooms marked "White" and "Colored" in the railroad stations down South, and we had to learn the subtle machinations of maintaining dignity in these situations. Assessing the vast racial discrepancy on most plantations as evidence, our mother told us that there were so many more colored than white people down South that the white people were afraid of being swallowed up, so they had decided to mark off their parts just for themselves.

Trains were really important in my parents' lives. People then didn't travel so regularly across the country in cars and vans the way they do now. It was mostly either the Greyhound or Trailways bus or the train. There was a palpable hierarchy around these modes of transportation, and in my parents' view of things decent people, if they could in any way afford it, took the train. Somehow bus journeys were fraught with potential trouble. There is only one time in my life that I can call to mind Day riding a Trailways bus. It's the only time I can ever remember being aware of the presence of fear in my mother, so the surrounding incidents are etched into my memory.

When I return to the time in my mind, I remember it as a particularly hot summer. The War is over, so I am ten or eleven years old, and for the first time our mother has allowed us to take a friend along on our trip Down Home. This little girl, Shirley, is just between the ages of my sister Audrey and me. Her mother,

Miss Ernestine, is one of the few really close friends my mother has ever had. Shirley, an only child, is such a close playmate that sometimes our mothers buy us all identical plaid dresses or matching deep blue swimsuits sprinkled with little stars.

We are having an exciting train trip, and Audrey and I are showing off our experience with the *City of New Orleans*, giggling and, when we reach Cairo, Illinois, mimicking the conductor's "May-son–Dixon Line." He never says that all of the colored people who have been sitting in the front cars of the train have to move now to the rear, but everybody knows it. The codes are inviolable. When we walk through the next car, a little tow-headed boy asks his mother, pointing, "M-M-Mama! Are those n-n-nig-gers?" "Yay-es dear," she says without perceptible affect. We mimic her later, laughing hilariously in my uncle's kitchen. It is all so palpably ridiculous to us, the Mason-Dixon Line, the little straw-haired boy with his stammering epithet, his mother with her pale-faced drawl. We are not bitter. We n-n-niggers are having a w-w-wonderful trip.

En route to catch the bus that will take us to my uncle's farm, we stop for a while to visit with distant cousins in McComb. They have a shiny modern kitchen and a bath with a real shower we take turns in. Their teenage son has a motorcycle and gives us rides one at a time. The other children love the vroom-vroom and the speed. I hate it and refuse a second ride.

Later the cousins leave us at the bus station and board a bus to Grenada. We wait out in the square playing invisible hop-scotch while our mother goes into a little station house to buy tickets for us to Woodville. When she comes back out, her face is pale and strained. She had been denied the right to buy tickets at the colored booth, turned away by a nervous-looking man who pointed her to the white side. Now she has also been denied the option to buy tickets at the white booth by a big red-faced man who pointed at us playing outside and shook his head. She explained, but neither would sell her tickets, and now she has come out, suddenly anxious.

She tries to get a taxi, but their taxis will not take colored people. She tells us to sit still on a bench directly outside the station. We are quiet. I have never before seen our mother seeming shaky. Something is happening that we don't understand. The men on the steps are chewing tobacco and spitting into the dust, and everything is feeling heavy, hot, inexplicable. Our mother approaches some of the men and speaks quietly, then comes to retrieve us. We walk slowly away from the square. At a dusty intersection, one of the men drives up in a car, old and dirty. Our mother lifts us into the back seat one at a time. She gets into the back seat, too, putting Audrey on her lap. The car's motor never stops running. That is the only sound until we reach our uncle's farm.

Our mother has paid the man one hundred dollars. It is all of the money she had. It was meant to pay for everything, including our train fare back to Chicago. Now the money is gone, but we are safe. Uncle Ben is enraged and wants to go hunt down the man and make him give the money back, and we children think he should. But our mother says, "No. It is over. We are okay."

Ten years later I read a scene in a Faulkner short story. In the story, red-necked men chewing tobacco watch a dog whose tail has been cut off as he runs in circles of agony. They just sit. I am pierced with the buried memory of my mother's fear.

I never liked going Down Home. First of all, before you even got close to the house, as soon as whatever four-wheeled vehicle was carrying you turned off the main road onto the winding dirt pathway, the dogs would start up to barking, and they would continue nonstop. I've no idea how many dogs there were, but it sounded to my city ears like about a hundred of them. Then there were the other animals. Chickens walked in and out of the house as though they had every right to, terrorizing me. I wasn't allowed to tuck both my feet under the seat of the highest chair I could find, as every nerve in my body was crying out that I should do. Horses were the worst. Our mother had been a fearless little girl, tough in body, mind, and spirit and a superb bareback rider, and she had little sympathy for the primordial dread I suffered at the thought of approaching one of the wild-eyed creatures in the horse barn. I had to allow myself to be cantered about once or twice on what they called the gentlest one, trembling all the while, and that would mollify everybody for the rest of the time we were there.

Those farm animals, prolific in number and diversity, were the scourge of my annual month in the country. Disgusting hogs slopped in their troughs and weird-looking billy goats, urged to chase us by my wild boy cousins, made the strangest of noises. Old MacDonald choruses don't begin to capture the threatening quality of that sound. And then there were the loud-honking geese with their flapping wings. Once my cousin Sam put one of these squawky creatures in the lap of our nine-year-old next-door neighbor, Shirley, who had come with us from Chicago and who, like me, did not take readily to these alien environs. She got a terrible attack of the shakes and trembled in my mother's arms for over an hour before she could be calmed.

At the bottom of my list were the cows. My mother had no romance about these, but she thought we should learn basic farm things, like milking. My brother and sister loved this activity and happily splashed the warm milk into silver pails. I shuddered at the whole idea and got away with just a gingerly pull at a teat or two before one of my cousins would get disgusted with me and take over. Thanking the Lord, I never drank a drop of milk until we got to McComb or New Orleans, where people had refrigerators and had their milk in ice-cold bottles like we did at home.

CHAPTER 12. *Streetcars*

It is the family that gives us a deep private sense of belonging. Here we first begin to have our self defined for us.

· HOWARD THURMAN

God, is America's dream big enough for me?
I who am poor, average, disabled, girl, Black, Brown, Native American, White?
Is America for me?

· MARIAN WRIGHT EDELMAN

The world was presented to all of the children in our house as a limitless feast for our delectation; we just had to learn the rules and avoid things that were bad for us. Dinner-table conversations addressed any and all agendas, and defending your point in that circle made you eligible for anybody's debate team. When I read Nelson Algren's stories of how ethnic families in Chicago's neighborhoods discouraged any dissent between children and parents, often by slapping a child's mouth shut, I came to realize that not all families were like ours.

Outside our house we were taught to be citizens of the world at large. What the generation of the sixties came to call multi-culturalism was nothing new to me. Streetcar sojourns to exotic places—other neighborhoods in Chicago—were structured to teach us confidence in locating routes to anywhere and to give us the tools to navigate in different settings. Dressed to the nines, we were taken on excursions to the Chicago Fair, the Railroad Fair, or whatever major event was on that year. We usually went on these outings with my mother, just the three youngest ones, and frequently just Audrey and I.

One summer Day had bought a bolt of pale yellow organdy and had made little two-piece dresses for the two of us, with peplums. We were saving them to surprise everybody at the end-of-summer Vacation Bible School program at Olivet Baptist—she always liked for us to make a special splash on such occasions. But then we begged to wear them to the Railroad Fair, so she relented, laughing that we looked like two lemon drops and cautioning us not to get our dresses dirty. We climbed in and out of short trains and long trains, looking with wonder at the elaborate red, velvet-covered seats in somebody or another's private car. Since we always took our own lunch on train rides Down Home, these up-close views of the dining car were seductive—we yearned ever after to *dine* on those crisp white tablecloths with nice dishes and heavy silver. Anyway, needless to say, at the Railroad Fair our mother bought us cotton candy, and we spoiled those beautiful yellow dresses with pink goo. We felt so terrible that I can still remember it. Day stayed up that night, removed the transgressive stiff pink sugar without leaving a stain, then reironed the peplums, and the next day we wore the dresses, as good as new, to Bible School. We were a big hit too.

Both of our parents loved the Railroad Fair. Our father took the boys on a separate excursion, telling them his own stories. Trains were of great importance to his memory system because he had lived in the country and lain awake so many nights listening to train whistles. Anything that moved on a track meant freedom to him, and later the automobiles he owned were his pride and joy, so when he died, we knew we had to bury him near a highway.

We used to ride the streetcar to the neighborhood around Lincoln and Belmont Avenues, where small and large German sausages hung in the windows of shops with signs written in an Old German script that reminded me then of my Grimm's fairy tale book, and where, though I cannot corroborate this, I could swear I remember glimpsing a banner with a swastika. Most Germans, of course, were desperate to separate themselves from Hitler, and so most shop windows bore American flags or posters saying "Bring Our Boys Home." We rode another streetcar line north to Swedish Andersonville, where it is always Christmas in my memory, and where we used to get off the streetcar to buy lacy cookies dusted with powdered sugar from bakeries that smelled impossibly good.

I had learned when riding the streetcar with my father through the streets around Milwaukee and North Avenue inhabited by those very Algrenesque families I read about later that the Polish people had staked out these streets as their territory and that it was more judicious for colored people to ride the streetcar through there than to drive or walk.

During my childhood, our father worked at a huge printing press factory that in those wartime years was given over to the manufacture of aircraft. It was located on the Near Southwest Side, near Cook County Hospital, and its workers were mainly recent Eastern European immigrants. Lacking formal education and grateful for remunerative work, few of this wary group ventured to talk much about the war, but the plant owners were very patriotic, and U.S. flags hung about the place along with war-effort posters.

Workers' children were invited annually to a Family Day, when we were given all of the hot dogs and soda pop we could imbibe, and when, best of all, we could climb up onto the airplanes. My father always prepared us carefully for these events, reminding us that many of the people there couldn't speak English as well as we could, might not yet have learned American ways, and might lack the careful manners and decorum we had mastered. I realized much later his ingenuity. He was armoring us ahead of time to cope with any racial insults like those he likely suffered in his daily work. On Family Day he ensured before the fact that we would receive any racist negativity as a sign of deficiency on *their* part, not ours. Such family strategies succeeded in laying a permanent foundation for inner strength and impregnability to other emotional assaults that American racism would visit upon us from time to time throughout our lives.

Chicago's celebrated ethnic diversity has always been fraught with racism. We were aware of the tensions, living as we did in a community bounded on the west by the mixed Italian/Irish neighborhood of Bridgeport and on the north by Chinatown, with Mexican Town immediately beyond. Our park district competitions pitted us against teams from their parks. Our library, Hardin Square, sat right on the borderline between our neighborhood and Bridgeport, as did Comiskey Park, where we regularly went to Chicago White Sox baseball games.

After Jackie Robinson and then Roy Campanella came to play with the Brooklyn Dodgers, we went up north to Wrigley Field to cheer them on. Racial discord would break out with some regularity at sporting events. When a black player was critical to his team's winning a game, or when a black player made a spectacular play, there were often sneering or catcalls from some white hoodlums. Mostly, black people took refuge in the undeniable skill and talents of our players and tried to ignore the sheer painful ugliness in these situations. Our parents talked derisively of the affronts, dismissing perpetrators as trash or worse. None of us had any illusions about the ever-present potential for racial challenges, but while we learned early to avoid head-on confrontations, we also learned to distinguish such offenders from other white people, with whom we experienced positive daily encounters. Most people we knew made clear distinctions among whites and blacks of different classes, maintained a sense of social superiority to white race-baiters, and thought it ironic when they characterized us as coming from a lower rung on the class ladder.

I am always surprised and dismayed when I read books about

the South Side that categorize our neighborhood as a deprived community, using a skewed terminology attributable only to deeply rooted white racism. In the 1940s and 1950s that I knew, as in the 1920s and 1930s of our parents' experience, the colored community occupied the best housing to be found for miles. Although there was certainly some overcrowding, especially near the State Street commercial strip, there were scores of nicely kept apartment buildings and lovely old houses, many now re-gentrified. In my childhood, the post-Depression competition for housing and jobs that had contributed to the most fierce racial tensions was still definitely present, but was somewhat diminished. Most people had jobs during the war, many worked double shifts, and everybody looked forward to a better life. Someone wrote recently that when the private, upscale apartment complexes of Lake Meadows and Prairie Shores were built in the mid-1950s, displaced residents moved farther south to other "ghettos." Families we knew, including our own, did move south to Park Manor and Chatham, but then as now these were neighborhoods of tree-lined streets; small, immaculate bungalows with garages; carefully kept lawns; and proud, hard-working residents.

Along the route I walked daily to my Near South Side high school just prior to the demolition of our neighborhood, there were doctors, dentists, and lawyers living in large, elegant gray-stones and red-brick townhouses. There were also factory workers and postal workers and men who "ran on the road," living in bright, airy apartments. When we children were sent to buy whipped cream birthday cakes from Dressel's in Bridgeport, the white neighborhood adjacent to the west, or to Chinatown to buy egg fu yung, the mostly wood-frame houses with little or no front yards seemed much smaller and poorer than many of those that lined our streets. Ironically, although we knew their neighborhood, they rarely came into ours. This enforced segregation might have been salutary. If there had been more communication among the races, there might have been even more serious anger. The history of the 1921 Tulsa, Oklahoma, race riots demonstrates how white envy of colored prosperity can foment and unleash rabid destruction by the white underclass.

What we children loved about those neighborhoods where we didn't live—we had no idea that we *couldn't* live there because we never wanted to—were the various culinary delights abounding on their foreign-seeming streets. In addition to the de rigueur Dressel's cakes and the cardboard cartons of strange-smelling things from Chinatown (which I, with my always extra-sensitive olfactory system, refused to eat, to the great satisfaction of my brothers, who wolfed down the extra portions), there were wonderful Italian beef and pepper sandwiches from Ricobene's near the ball park, and we were taken on some occasions to Mexican Joe's farther north, where you could order your chili hot or extra-hot (no mild on the chalkboard menu), and with or without grease.

My older siblings loved Mexican Joe's and liked all of the people who worked there. One cold afternoon in late November 1968, we gathered there in grief. It was a week or so after our brother Jay had died, and some one of his legions of friends had arranged for a Mass to be said for his soul. After the Mass we went into our several cars and drove almost on radar to Mexican Joe's to sit in his crowded back booth and tell yet again the stories that we hoped would bind us together in this new way, reconstitute us as a family still, four now instead of five, as we bled with the unbearable wounds of Jay's absence. We had extra-hot chili, with grease. Mexican Joe wouldn't let us pay for anything, and the waiters, solemn, shook our hands when we left.

CHAPTER 13. *In the Castle of Our Skin*

They couldn't conceive for a moment the land as being other than a village, and on reflection, the threat to a whole village seemed ridiculous.

· GEORGE LAMMING

Although the boys had definitely been a unit, with a bond between them that nothing could break, the youngest three of us were another kind of cohort. Arthur, Audrey, and I were together a great deal during the war years, while Zoe and Jay occupied a more adult space. Day talked about it this way:

I raised all five of my children to be close to one another and to be responsible to each other like in that book I used to read to them, The Five Little Peppers. *My two brothers had always made me feel protected, and I had looked up to them, so I wanted that for my own girls. With Zoe being the oldest, she became a little like a mother, though not quite, of course. She was such a pretty girl it would have been easy for her to be centered on herself a lot, but she was never like that. She and Jay always had real good times together but were always mindful of the younger children, teaching them how to be, in ways that a mother or father couldn't do.*

Your father and I always said that the older two made our job easier. They helped you all with your homework, and they helped to make it clear for all of you what the difference was between right and wrong because they were smart and popular and they both came home on time. We never seemed to have to punish our children much—your father got the message across from the beginning that parents set the rules, that's for sure, and as the older children grew up, you younger ones just wanted to be like them. Still, Zoe was born with a temper, and sometimes she and your father would have a set-to, usually about his being too strict—sometimes he didn't listen when he should have. Then all of you would line up on her side, and he would just have to leave well enough alone and go in the kitchen and read the paper until everybody cooled off. I had a hard way to go sometimes trying to respect my husband as head of the family and still give my children respect too, and enough room to grow up straight and strong.

As each of the older children grew up enough to hold down some kind of job—they started working a few hours a week while still in high school—they would buy you all presents, little fancy things like a special scarf or a locket, or a leather wallet with picture holders in it. Best of all, I thought then and I still think so, were the Saturday morning times when everybody sat around together and just laughed and talked. I miss those times, and as I grow older, I realize how precious those days were. Nobody had anywhere as much money as people do today, nobody had their own room, just a girls' room and a boys' room and one bathroom for everybody, but maybe having to live so close up on one another was a good thing. There wasn't enough privacy for any one person to get into trouble, so you might just as well all get along and care for one another.

We adored our older sister and brother without question. They dressed up—Zoe wore high wedgie shoes, fishnet stockings, and Evening in Paris perfume, and Jay wore peg leg pants and houndstooth jackets and polished his Florsheims to a manly gleam. They went out with Zoe's boyfriend Pat to the Club De Lisa, where they drank sloe gin fizzes and got their pictures taken looking fabulously grown-up, and they frequented the Savoy Ballroom, where they danced to live bands. Along with our parents, we younger three thrilled to their recounting as they sat on our beds on Saturday or Sunday mornings and told us all about these dazzling evenings. Best of all, they gave us souvenir swizzle sticks, which we would show off to our friends.

Each of we younger three assumed responsibility for the others, as we were taught. Our brother Arthur, four years older than I but just two years ahead in school (I had skipped some grades) was my protector. When I was a very small girl, he carried me on his shoulders across the Illinois Central tracks to the lake. (I wonder if our mother knew this!) During the war, it was Arthur who every week loaded our red wagon full with newspapers and pulled it to the collection center at school. We usually had the most papers of anyone in the neighborhood, since our family habit was to read morning and evening editions of the city dailies plus the weekly *Chicago Defender*. Arthur was himself a Saturday morning *Defender* delivery boy, and Audrey and I occasionally accompanied him as he belted out "Cah-go Defen-do" to attract customers. Among us children we giggled another ditty, though *never* in the hearing of adults, except our own parents, who were gamemakers surpassed by none: "Lady, lady, with your bald-headed baby, stick your head out the window, holler 'Cah-go Defen-do.'"

At a later age, Arthur commanded the loyalties of his gang of friends to teach me to ride a boy's two-wheeled bicycle, and still later, when I was fourteen, to persuade one of his friends to accompany me on a double date to the Regal Theater. My memory of this latter occasion is still excruciating: Our mother had helped me to dress up for what, as she saw it, was my first foray into the world of courting. I wore an aqua silk-satin dress with a Peter Pan collar, pearls, and wobbly high heels. Arthur's date, a gorgeous edition of the kind of high-breasted, self-confident Catholic school girls he favored, wore a plaid pleated wool skirt, a soft blue cashmere sweater, and loafers. Visibly *wrong*, I was mortified and uncharacteristically tongue-tied. I couldn't *look* at that nice boy, whose name was Donald, for the rest of our high school years. Still, I learned a lot about boys and dating from my big brother, and within a year or so I had pretty much mastered the game.

Adolescent mating rituals were a lot easier then than now, and our crowd was, by today's standards, wholesome beyond belief. We had lots of parties, city hayrides (in an open truck), swimming parties at the Wabash Y, and weekend dances in our high-school gym. No drugs, no liquor, very little smoking. Audrey's experience a few years later was similar to mine. She was part of a tight-knit club called the Shamrocks, where boys and girls got together regularly as an informal group. I was a "sponsor" for her club and in this way served as mentor, extending into my early twenties the teenage pleasures I had otherwise largely foregone.

Married at the tender age of seventeen, I had graduated from the University of Chicago at nineteen and had gotten a job working in a publishing company downtown. We didn't call it a career in those days, just a job. For our mother, my graduation from *The* university (as she called it years before latter-day university president Hannah Gray entered that term firmly in the U of C lexicon) was an acknowledgment of what she and our surrounding community had predicted when I was a small child—that I would accomplish something special intellectually. Our family would inhabit that place because I was there. When Day came to watch me receive my degree, she dressed for the occasion in a white "chubby" jacket and a white hat with a feather.

Arthur was then serving in the U.S. Army Medical Corps in Okinawa, and when he returned, burned by the sun and four inches taller, and thus nearly unrecognizable, he brought elaborately embroidered satin Japanese pajamas as gifts for each of his sisters. He knew that our mother would eschew such exotica, so he brought her a simpler cotton *yukata*. She was pleased at the gift, but she found it too foreign still, so she kissed him, thanked him for it, and then kept it folded in her bottom dresser drawer, whence we retrieved it, unworn, after she died.

Audrey was our baby, and with no younger one as her charge, she too took on responsibility for me. More outspoken than I, she often took my part, vocally sparring with other kids, even those much bigger than herself. She had what our father called spunk, and whenever she thought I was being taken advantage of in any way, she put a quick stop to it. One summer when we were among the first of the neighborhood little girls to get a bicycle, everybody wanted to take turns riding it. For Audrey this got out of control, and she drew up a plan: we would limit the loaning of the bike to three days a week, reserving the other days for uninterrupted family-only exploring. Since she explained these rules with total authority and firmness, as well as open good humor, they were accepted readily by the other children, and she and I were assured long bicycling days. The surrounding neighborhoods were safe and had little traffic, and we took turns, each of us riding for miles on end.

This executive management of our bicycle time was entirely characteristic of Audrey from her earliest years. A born leader, she managed endless activities for her own crowd of friends and, when necessary, for mine. Countering my tendency to let things go their own way, her inclination was always to create a structure and then to persuade people to implement it. It was no surprise to anyone of the family that Audrey became a highly successful executive director and financial planner. Of all of us, Audrey is the most like our mother in acuity and decisiveness, in consistent fairness and open-mindedness. Also like our mother, she is generous always with sound advice and advances of money when anybody needs it.

When we were little girls, resplendent in our pastel Sunday dresses and Shirley Temple curls, we were trotted in for the edification and admiration of family friends. My father always had some fact or another he wanted us to declaim for the group: "Girls, come in here and inform these gentlemen about the original thirteen colonies," he would say, smiling in the sure knowledge that we would never embarrass him. Audrey and I would reel off the names of all those states and their capitals without missing a beat, pleased to confirm our father's own reputation for being smarter than everybody, and knowing that the men would listen to us respectfully and say, "Well, Rone, these children surely do have brains. From their mother's side, of course," Then there was the second reason we looked forward to their gatherings: they gave us quarters. Audrey would almost always put hers in her big, old 1933 World's Fair bank, but I always spent mine pretty quickly on notebooks with red, yellow, or blue shiny covers. Or sometimes on Pink Passion nail polish or movie popcorn. This history is for me a clear indication that adults are pretty much the same as they were when they were in first grade. While Audrey grew up to be a successful financial manager, I still spend too much money on pedicures and potato chips. Which inclination is from our mother's side and which from our father's side is pretty clear within the family, where both sides are honored equally.

We were honored not only by our family, but also by certain exemplary neighbors, and we respected them equally. In the world of our close-knit community, the relationship between children and older adults was a well-defined, carefully tended, and profoundly respectful dialogue. Certain memories of one particular old lady, Miss Hill—we never knew her first name, emerge sharply from those years, and my brother, sister, and I find ourselves talking about her with some frequency. In some regards, the cultural appurtenances that surrounded her were much the shaping stuff of our small lives, and looking back, they held so many inherent lessons.

Miss Hill had white hair, braided neatly, not in today's fashionable neo-Africanist styles, but simply, like a little girl's. Her skin was dark and soft, her back was bent, and she wore immaculate aprons over her long skirts. Her hands were in perpetual nervous motion, in and out of numberless deep pockets that held her essential things—a tin of Garrett Sweet snuff, a clean handkerchief wrapped around a dollar and fastened with a rubber band or two, a few red and white striped peppermints, a couple of buffalo nickels (that's what she—and we—called them), and maybe a leather-covered book of the Psalms. I knew about the book of Psalms because once in a while she would retrieve it from one of her pockets and read me a few lines, slowly, to illustrate something she thought I should know.

I felt important because Miss Hill thought I was *interesting*. I had a neighborhood reputation for having learned to read at age three, and Miss Hill liked that. She thought reading was a great thing, and she observed me and my sister Audrey staggering up the stairs with our weekly pile of library books from the Hardin Square branch. (This beautiful little library in a park later disappeared under the wrecker's ball to make way for the Dan Ryan Expressway. It was not replaced, but by then I had gone on and was borrowing my weekly stack of books from another library, down at the University of Chicago.) Miss Hill observed a lot. Her sharp, bright eyes didn't miss much, especially not the carryings-on of people who lived in the building we lived in.

As children we were interested in Miss Hill because she seemed to be always there, standing around in the building lobby or sitting in an old chair in front. She shared a small, very neat apartment on the first floor with her brother, Mr. Hill, who was a less important part of our lives. He had a face half eaten away by cancer of the jaw, and he had blue eyes. Maybe they were the result of cataracts—we didn't know about things like that then—but I think they were just blue eyes, surprising as they peered out of his dark-skinned face, like those I saw years later in Paul Strand's African photographs. Miss Hill took care of Mr. Hill, and we ran errands for both of them. We ran two blocks to bring them the *Herald American* evening edition, and sometimes we brought them a red and white paper bag of peanuts, roasted in their shells. The street corner vendor at 31st and Lake Park Avenue would put a bag in one of our hands with the top carefully folded and instruct us *not* to eat any but to take the bag *as is* to Miss Hill.

Mostly we honored requests such as this. I've no idea why. What people used to call home training, I suspect. We never cheated her and she never cheated us—we knew we could count on the nickel she gave us for running the errand.

How she came by her small sustenance, I never knew, nor did I wonder about it. Was there a thing called welfare then in those early postwar years? Did she have a pension, or a small nest-egg from a tiny house sold in Louisiana or Alabama? Did Mr. Hill get a regular check from some form of government assistance for his cancer of the jaw? What schooling had they had? I never knew, but Miss Hill spoke clear, lucid English, peppered with metaphor. They didn't converse at length with us, really, but were simply there at the edges of our world. The Hills were these old people. We were children with responsibilities to them, in another time, on the South Side of Chicago.

We ran to Mr. Ross's grocery store around the corner and across the street and brought back Scott's toilet paper and Lipton's tea, a can of Clabber Girl baking powder or two cans of Niblets corn, self-importantly putting the charge on the bill; Miss Hill would pay sometime, we never knew or cared how or when. The worn buffalo nickel we were given for our trouble would buy a sharp, cold sour pickle or a popsicle, or an immensely satisfying writing tablet with sheets of pink and blue. In season, a nickel would purchase a pomegranate, seductive with the promise of pulpy scarlet seeds inside, to be eaten slowly and carefully while sitting on the steps watching the world go by. Miss Hill would thank us courteously and caution us not to leave popsicle wrappers or pomegranate peel on the steps, reminding us of our manners. She herself had wonderful manners. Although she smiled only in fragments, she had a calm, quiet demeanor, not so much gentle as composed. As I think of it now, what Miss Hill had was dignity. And she helped to ensure, for us children, a certain order in our world, that wider world outside of our parents and siblings.

CHAPTER 14. *Dining In*

In these hands
I could trust the world, or in many hands like these,
. . . Such hands could turn
the unborn child rightways in the birth canal.

· ADRIENNE RICH

Such tenderness, those afternoons and evenings,
saying *blackberry, blackberry, blackberry.*

· ROBERT HASS

Day Shepherd was something of a loner and kept her contact with her adult neighbors to a minimum. Many of them thought she was a white woman living with a colored man, and if she wanted to pass for colored, well nobody cared. There were others in the neighborhood like that.

Just out our back door, on the other side of South Parkway, was a neat two-flat owned by a colored family, the Nesbitts. Mr. Nesbitt was the assistant principal at our high school and known to be a strict disciplinarian and a sharp dresser. His wife was a soft-spoken, motherly woman who, when I was a small child, supervised the girls' activities at our playground. An important mentor to me and to many of us who were not sports-minded, she would gather us in her office when we shied away from the softball field, and there we would talk for hours about our lives, hopes, and possibilities—and Mrs. Nesbitt thought all things were possible for us.

The family who shared the Nesbitts' building were the Wards. Mr. Ward was a white man with a slender, elegant, brown-skinned wife and a cute freckle-faced daughter called Twinkle. It seemed unimportant to anybody around that Twinkle had a white father. What was more important for me was that they had a piano, which Mrs. Ward allowed me to play when I visited them. There was also blue-eyed Carolyn, down across the street from our school, whose father was white. And everybody loved a sunny, open-faced little girl named Jackie, whose mother was white and father was Filipino. There were two half-Mexican, half-black families within a block or two, one with a Mexican mother who taught me how to make tortillas, and the other with a sober, stern Mexican father who I never remember saying anything to us.

There were also white people on the block who were not visibly related to anybody of color. A white family owned the school store at the end of the street, and their little boy was in my class. He never seemed to be treated differently from anybody else. Across the street on the corner was a dilapidated wooden house largely shaded from view by trees and unkempt hedges and lilac bushes that flowered profusely in spring, perfuming the air all about. We called the old white woman who lived there a hermit, and she chased us kids away when we got too near her yard. For some reason I have never understood, however, she took a certain liking to me and would beckon me to her fence to fill my arms with lilacs when they were in season.

We also had at least two teachers with racially mixed families. Although they did not live immediately nearby, their several colored children attended our school with their mothers, who as far as we could tell were white—a distinction we made on the basis less of color than of styles of speaking. On occasion one teacher or another would ask us outright if our mother was white or colored. We were taught to answer that if they had personal questions, they should ask our parents. No one ever did, as far as I knew. Such relative racial harmonies, which seem to be no longer viable in many places, were normative in our neighborhood. For the most part, questions of race were secondary. Judgments were made according to how well a woman kept her children and her house, how a man managed his family, and whether children were mannerly and respectful to their elders.

Our mother did encourage our relationships with certain of the neighbor children. Our regular dinner guests included a shy girl of my age named Polly, who had very long, exquisitely straightened hair. Thin as the proverbial rail, she was an only child reared by a silent, meek-seeming woman who was not her mother but an aunt or cousin. Polly was very quiet herself. The very walls of the apartment they occupied seemed to breathe silence—and we were always more than a bit uncomfortable on the rare occasions when we tiptoed into the neat stillness of their kitchen.

I have two distinct recollections of Polly. One was that she always covered her mouth when she laughed, like a grownup, stifling the sound. That was in marked contrast to the general hilarity and open noisiness of children in our neighborhood. Secondly, although Polly was frequently excluded by many of the children our age, I liked her quite enough and I was utterly fascinated by the strange solitariness of her life. I couldn't really imagine a home with fewer than a half-dozen people in it. Once I watched, riveted, as Polly's aunt prepare her supper, her subdued movements given to opening a tiny can of Niblets corn and another tiny can of Vienna sausages, heating them on a small stove, and arranging them carefully on a plain cream-colored plate. After I shared this scenario with my mother, Polly became a frequently invited guest at our prodigious and wildly conversational dinner table, and she maintained her sweetly smiling silence throughout. My father praised her exquisite manners, but her quiet acted as a wall—she was of no interest whatsoever to my brothers, either to show off for or to tease.

Another intermittent dinner guest was the direct opposite of

Polly. Diane was a short, muscular girl with snapping black eyes and a blunt, confrontational manner. Helping herself directly to the fragrant dishes my mother passed around, she was the kind of child who, as my parents said, made herself very much at home. She was not a particular friend of mine — too athletic and too much of a tomboy for me. The thing was that Diane was another loner, and my parents had an unspoken openness to including such children in our circle. Too, they admired Diane's toughness: my brother Arthur teased her, but not too much, because she was the only girl we knew who would fight with boys in a minute. One or another of my brothers' friends, Fred or Snookie or Goldbaby, whose extremely well-behaved sister Peaches was in my class, came to dinner occasionally too, and they comported themselves perfectly, respecting our mother and fearing our father. This was in radical opposition to their behavior on the schoolyard, and it showed us girls a different side of these rambunctious little boys, making them secretly interesting to us.

Dinner was one of the most significant daily rituals that bound our family together. First of all, it was as regular as clockwork. Decades later sociological studies began to emphasize the long-term positive impact of regular family meals, but at that time no one ever thought about it as something "good for the children." Rather, we always thought that my mother's emphasis on the daily table was required by my father and constructed to coincide exactly with his arrival home from work, dividing the day evenly into two parts.

My father got home at 5:15 five days a week, with the exception of some Fridays, when he would stop to celebrate payday, especially if it was an overtime week. A very fastidious man, he would come in and bathe immediately (my mother would have his hot bath already drawn) to remove the printing-press ink that stained his hands and arms. Perhaps that ink stained his soul as well, for he underwent daily small indignities at work. Day saw it as her personal responsibility to correct all of that, and she did.

When Dray Rone came home from work the first thing he did was to change his clothes. I would always have laid out a clean ironed shirt and underwear on our big double bed. You youngest girls would have already cleaned up for dinner—in the summer when you all played outside almost all day, you had to come inside to be bathed before your father set eyes on you. Then you two set the table every day except Sundays. I would give you a clean, ironed tablecloth and napkins to arrange orderly—I love a nice orderly place. You would set the plates and Audrey would set the glasses, because we all knew you were the clumsier one and Audrey took more after my side of the family. Her ways always reminded me of Mama Emmaline's. Both of you would be responsible for the silver. Of course, it was not really silver, but just a stainless steel sixty-four-piece service for eight.

Real silver is not for everyday use. It makes Christmas, Easter, and Thanksgiving special, and it shines up a celebration like when one of you would win a prize, or at your graduation. Because you, my middle girl, have always been the fancy type, you were always looking for some reason to lay out the real silver, and you have my love of flowers, too. We were lucky that you could clip them from that old lady Miz Lewis's overgrown bushes. You had the nicest way of putting out a bunch of spring lilacs and setting them in wine goblets right in the center of the table.

The family was fondly accepting of my innate predilection for the aesthetic, and my mother decided well before she died to leave her real silverware, which had always resided in a mahogany tarnish-proof box, to me. Her explanation to everybody was that her other two girls had their own silver, having had large weddings, which I had not. She understood that this one of her girls had a special affection for fancy things, and thought that it would be a shame if someone with my inclinations couldn't have that silver. Not to put too fine a point on it, she also knew that I could be a bit cavalier when it came to the actual demands of household maintenance, and so she admonished me seriously about proper antitarnish care.

It is still a source of pain and shame to me that years after she died I lost several of her forks (and that is how I think of them even now—as hers) while transporting them in a wicker basket to one of those elegant concert picnics. Disastrously, I had ignored the fact that our basket had once been bitten through by a raccoon on some camping trip or another. I might have gotten over blaming myself for this slovenliness with more psychic ease had it not been so predictable. Along with the fanciness of my father's side, I exhibited his regrettably characteristic carelessness about some things. Still I could just see my mother smiling in forgiveness as she shook her head at me. It was Day's understanding that each person was culpable in some particular ways and not without specific vulnerabilities, usually attributable to heredity from some known or unknown forebear. She thus rendered our foibles largely unavoidable and therefore more or less acceptable.

Another silver story in the family revolves around our mother's always evident understanding of the diverse ways of her children. She had a beautiful three-piece silver-plated tea set, one of those now anachronistic symbols of careful housekeeping that in another time gleamed on each home's sideboard, polished to a T. This set was never actually used, to my knowledge, except once, and that was at a grand party my mother gave for Zoe when she got her degree from Chicago Teachers College.

Zoe's graduation from Teacher's College meant more to me than those of all of the rest of my children combined. My prize of a first daughter had put off her college studies in favor of getting married at the age of nineteen. Now here it was! She had gone back to school, two or three classes at a time, and her succeeding was just that more delicious because it was belated. I was determined to prepare a lavish party for this celebration, so I put flowers everywhere, baked a ham and roasted a turkey, and laid out my special recipe for orange and coconut ambrosia. I polished up Zoe's silver punch bowl and filled that up with white wine and strawberries. I knew how to put out a spread, and I wouldn't let anybody help with this party—it was a triumph for my firstborn girl. I wanted to do this by myself. If there was an event worthy of my silver tea service, this was it, so I polished it inside and out and served the real thing—actual English Breakfast tea. We never had tea much in our house or at any of my cousins, being Louisiana coffee people, but I knew how to serve it right, with little tiny cubes of sugar; real cream, not half-and-half; and a silver plate of the thinnest, most perfect lemon slices.

When our sister Zoe died, years after our mother's penultimate tribute to her, we all sat around telling stories, and that one story was so rich with our mother's spirit and with our memories of all the toasting for Zoe, with her serious dark eyes and luminous, movie-star smile, that we all wept. We laughed, too, remembering how when my mother distributed her worldly goods the year before she died, she gave that silver tea service to Zoe. Since Zoe already had her own perfectly fine tea service occupying a place of honor on her own antique walnut sideboard, this might have seemed an odd decision. But my mother announced to everyone that she had these three daughters, and there were these facts to be reckoned with: First, Audrey, the youngest, had inherited a tea service from her mother-in-law and kept it polished but sitting on a shelf behind glass doors in a lighted-up china cupboard. Second, if it were left to her middle girl, she would just put dried flowers and leaves in it. It was her thinking that only Zoe would treat Day's tea service right, so Zoe ended up with it, and it then assumed the central place on the buffet. Zoe's wedding tea set was given to her son Skippy and his bride. People outside the family might question this, but the family understood unanimously.

CHAPTER 15. *Go Down the Street*

Bright lameness from my beautiful disease,
You have your destiny to chip and eat.

Be precise.
With something better than candles in the eyes.
(Candles are not enough.)

At the roof of the will, a wild and flammable stuff.

New pioneers of days and ways, be gone.
Hunt out your own or make your own alone.

Go down the street.

· GWENDOLYN BROOKS

The rivers of memory bear my childhood back to me, colors and patterns merging on the surface of my consciousness, meanings to be probed in the shifting silt of family experience. At one shore I return to the traditional rituals of our lives, the simple quotidian regularities of shopping. Our mother guided whatever children accompanied her, usually the youngest three, in and out of a half-dozen storefront businesses, always ensuring that we had the absolute best selections from every greengrocer and butcher, poultry store and shoe store, and the small, dark dry-goods shop that had the widest variety of ribbons and laces.

Our mother was the scourge of tradesmen like Meyer, the local butcher, who once asked our mother outright if she was Jewish. She told him that she considered that a personal question and that he needed to stick to his business: "Your business is not my race, Meyer. Your business is meat." He never raised the question again. She wouldn't accept anything but his very best cuts of meat, and she would firmly refuse to pay for one fraction of an ounce more than absolutely called for, insisting that he remove his finger from anywhere near the scale. He didn't dare cheat her, or any of us children either, but would shake his head in appreciation, saying, "Your mother is *some* lady."

The same combination of exasperation and admiration was evident whenever we were taken to buy shoes (and this was on a relentless rotation—new school shoes first week of September and second week of February; new patent leather Sunday shoes at Easter and at Christmas; white open-toed sandals and what we called tennis shoes as soon as school let out.) After examining all of the shoes in the window of Jackie's Shoe Store on 31st and Calumet, we would walk in and settle into one of the rows of hard chairs to wait for our moment. Back then when you tried on the first new pair, you would place first one foot and then the other into an X ray machine. Peering into its small window, you could see the exact bones of your own foot in neon-green illumination. We absolutely loved this machine. Not to be rushed, Day's children tried on dozens of pairs of shoes before a decision was forthcoming. Sometimes we occupied Jackie's for an hour, wearing the salesman down to frazzled resignation.

It was the same story at the live poultry store. I hated going anywhere near there because of the distinctly sour smell emanating from the door. Once inside, I had to confront its other fact: the chickens had genuinely weird eyes. In our childish imaginations, we fantasized that the chickens were plotting how to get back at the people who bought them for the horrible purpose of plucking, cooking, and eating them. Our mother would allow me to wait outside if I chose to, which I mostly did.

Totally fearless, my mother would pick up a chicken by its neck, feel its breast to see if it would have enough meat on its bones, and put it back in disgust if it didn't meet her standards. Sometimes she would try out a half-dozen chickens this way, orange-feathered ones that looked like calico cats, or pullets with black and white patterned feathers. Finally the chicken man, defeated, would shuffle to the back of the store and pull out two of the best, most exemplary chickens from his secret stash, and my mother would hold each in both hands, one at a time, and say, "Well, now, there's a *bird*." Later, at home, she would without guilt wring the chickens' necks, singe the feathers, clean the birds to the nth degree, season them well, and then fry them up in the tenderest buttermilk batter imaginable.

Her platters of golden chicken were universally prized, and whenever someone died, their family would make the expected request: Can Day bring a couple of her special fryers for the repast? Modest about most things, she enjoyed her reputation as a fine cook and was generous with her culinary gifts. On other occasions fortunate friends were treated to huge feasts of chicken étouffée that rivaled anything in New Orleans and to a nearly unbearably rich gumbo redolent of chicken, shrimp, and andouille sausage that my brother now tries with fair success to emulate. After all of us were married, our mother would invite us, with our grateful spouses and her grandchildren, to regular Sunday suppers. Now, in turn, we invite our next generation, but none of us has ever really mastered the Day chicken magic.

We didn't master our mother's Wonder Woman approach to housecleaning, either. Growing up motherless, Day had taken on womanly chores early, helping her grandmother with the planning and preparation of meals and with the multiple tasks associated with keeping their small wooden house so clean that you could eat off its floors. Somewhere along the way she must have vowed to herself that if she ever had children of her own they would *never* have to do all of those chores. Our few regular jobs were highly codified. The boys were assigned to taking out the garbage daily and washing the windows on a regular cycle. This latter they finished off by polishing the panes with old newspapers to a shine in which they—and our mother—could take pride. The girls had the tasks of setting and clearing the evening dinner table, and washing, drying, and putting away the dinner dishes. Our pride was in the hot-water rinsing that ensured the gleam of our everyday Sears Roebuck glassware.

Somewhere along the way one of the women Day worked for in their homes when she needed extra money had given her a set of amethyst-colored real crystal fluted wine and champagne glasses. They were rarely used, but from time to time we washed and dried them, too, then reinstalled them on a top shelf in the cupboard. After I had children, these eerie Northern echoes of a plantation Big House were boxed up and given to me, and I use some of them still, musing over their history.

Our mother, without visible effort, kept our too-small apartment in exquisite order, with double sets of ironed sheets and pillowcases on all of our beds, changed every week for a fresh pair. Her kitchen pantry shelves were lined with bright-flowered oil cloth and displayed identical tall, clear jars of sugar, flour, rice, and cornmeal. There were smaller jars of spaghetti and macaroni (we didn't call it pasta in those days) and a shelf of spice tins and jars, which we were taught not to put away until every sticky fingerprint had been wiped off.

We were never given to understand the *how* of our mother's housekeeping. She never wanted us to know how hard she worked at making our family life so seamless. Somehow, it all got done—more or less invisibly. She never seemed hurried or tired, and it was only after I had a large family of my own that I came to be truly awed at her accomplishment of the trillion small everyday tasks called for in keeping house, the dusting and polishing, the sweeping and scrubbing. I do remember coming home from school to sit in the kitchen and have coffee with my mother, and sometimes there would be yesterday's newspapers spread neatly on the floor, signaling that the linoleum was newly mopped, though we rarely actually *witnessed* her at this kind of work. There were sometimes curtain-stretchers lining the hallways of our apartment; they were used to ensure that our cream-colored lace curtains would hang perfectly straight at the living room bay windows.

My mother had no patience with the way some people's curtains hung crooked or were frayed at the edges, and she dismissed the Venetian blinds that were just then coming into fashion. Still, she was characteristically and endlessly open to her children's wants. When I was a high school sophomore and it was my turn to host the meeting of the dozen or so very proper young ladies making up the Delta Tri-Hi-Y, I pleaded desperately for new Venetian blinds for our glass-paneled front door, protesting that our familiar lace curtains were impossibly old-fashioned. My mother actually allowed me to go out to Goldblatt's department store and buy the blinds, and my brother Arthur was drafted to install them just in time for the meeting. He demanded the reward of serving as doorman so that he could assess the variously charming girls as they entered.

Might any other mother have flatly refused to allow her newly sophisticated, know-it-all fourteen-year-old daughter to redecorate her house? If a mother did accede to such a whim, wouldn't that daughter be required at the very least to assume the onerous responsibility of the upkeep of those blinds? How did Day handle it? She showed off the new blinds to everybody, saying with motherly pride that it was all the children's wonderful idea, and hadn't her second son done a beautiful job of installing them? Then she just added the Soilax cleaning of those blinds to her regular housekeeping schedule, and nobody ever realized that they were extra work.

I never heard our mother utter the phrase "waste not, want not," but she was preternaturally prudent in the use of resources. When our lace curtains became worn, she ripped them apart into ribbons of lace. Over many midnights, she sewed them into beautiful trimmings that transformed our Sears Roebuck penny-plain cotton slips and underpants into fine lingerie, shaping in us a sense of entitlement that she was committed we should have.

We came home from school each day taking for granted the pristine orderliness of our lives. On Mondays, washing days, the sheets would be hung on clotheslines in our big kitchen, and we helped, sometimes, to fold them. My mother's mathematically precise eye-hand coordination, passed on to Audrey and Arthur, unhappily eluded me. She could fold a sheet in half, take a corner, whip it across in one swift motion to the other corner, and then refold it perfectly four-square. The clumsiness I inherited from somewhere else was tolerated more or less patiently. My sheet corners *never* came out even; hers never came out crooked. But she would just say, "I had to learn early to do this. You won't have to, so don't worry about it." On Tuesdays she would have the ironing board up and would press the stacked sheets so our skin wouldn't be scratched. Mostly the children didn't iron, though when I was in high school and wanted my cotton summer skirts to be totally wrinkle-free, Day finally taught me how to do it. Still, most often, she ironed our clothes, encouraging us to spend our time with social activities or doing homework. On Wednesdays my sisters and brothers and I had club meetings or other activities, and I think that must have been a big Wonder Woman cleaning day.

Thursdays she usually had one of her cousins over or went to visit them. When I was in high school, she worked away from home on some days, taking on odd jobs to make extra money. Fridays, my father's payday, were the most wondrous days because we had special end-of-the-week dinners. When Audrey and I were very small girls, during the war, Day used to send us regularly on Fridays to meet my father at the Cottage Grove streetcar. He would step off the car, tall and handsome, waving at us, and take each of us by the hand, promising treats from the brown bag he had under his arm. We felt important, not suspecting one dimension of my mother's intention: People got paid in cash in those days, and feeling flush for a few minutes, as my mother would say, Dray Rone was known for being tempted away from his regular routine and stopping to treat his friends to a drink before coming upstairs with a considerably lighter wallet. Remembering the moonshine days, Day knew that our innocent presence was tacit insurance that our father would arrive at her dinner table on time.

Also when I was very small, before Zoe got married to her childhood sweetheart, Pat, she was assigned to wash the Friday dishes, and I would dry them and put them on the table for her to put away. I just loved it when she did the dishes, because she sang all the popular songs as she washed, and she would let me join in. Our mother rarely sang, though she did hum rather tunelessly as she went about her work. Increasingly hard of hearing from her mid-thirties on, she wore her hair over her ears, covering an old-fashioned hearing aid. She loved to hear us sing, though, and would often come into the kitchen and clap along in rhythm while her girls sang together.

I learned all the words to *Cielito Lindo* before I knew what the Spanish language was, and all the funny wartime songs in marching cadence—"I don't know / but I've been told, / Alaskan girls are mighty cold," and "All the while you can't come home, / Jody's got your girl and gone." Then there was the one about all the girls in France who didn't wear underpants, a forbidden thought. Day, who had always had a naive, childlike delight in naughty lyrics, would roll her eyes at these ditties. Those were Billy Eckstine days, too—we had every one of his records. Zoe sang his songs, like "I'll Be Loving You Always" and "Blue Skies," and when President Jack Kennedy made the latter song popular again, I was transported back across the years to my mother's kitchen, with my idolized oldest sister so in love with Pat and dreaming of being a bride.

When we were very small children, Pat had been our paperboy. He delivered the evening *Herald-American*, so he had been in our lives like a brother almost since anybody could remember. Pat had been born in Havana, Cuba, which we thought very exotic. The oldest of ten, he was called Cito by his family, who lived across the street. His father, originally from India, was a pharmacist who had moved to Panama and married a devoutly Catholic mixed-race woman. After they moved to Cuba and then the United States and settled on our street, their West Indian mother was always more than a little stand-offish from the rest of the neighborhood, keeping her six boys close, and always extremely protective of her four pretty girls. One, Marcelle, actually looked very much like Zoe and vied with her for neighborhood approbation as the most beautiful. Because all of Pat's family were Catholic and went to St. James Church nearly every single day, after a while Zoe began to go to Mass frequently too, wearing a black lace mantilla pinned to her hair with pearly combs from the dime store. Our mother had little patience with the whole Roman Catholic Church, or any other, really, but if Zoe wanted to go, well, that was okay with her. And so, with loyalty and admiration for Zoe, ultimately all of us came to be Roman Catholics, in the Rone family way, that is.

We were definitely a different kind of Catholic family. Although the five of us Rone children, lined up in the pew, constituted a cohort of sorts, neither our mother nor our father ever attended Mass. This peculiarity was noted unfavorably by the priests and nuns, as well as by certain parishioners who never missed the opportunity to question us, albeit piously, about our parents' absence. There was also the fact that we did not fit neatly into any familiar categories. The relatively small number of Catholic families of color in our little neighborhood were frequently from Puerto Rico or were immigrants, like Pat's family, from Panama, Cuba, or other former Spanish and French colonies in the Caribbean, so Catholicism, for us, always had an aura of the foreign, the esoteric. Their children were steeped in what they called the True Church, and they loved their part in all of it, the kneeling and genuflecting, the smoky incense and solemn processionals. Instead of the elaborate, flower-covered hats favored by the Baptists, their mothers adorned themselves with heavy lace veils and seemed to us more serious and devout than we could ever be. We were fascinated by their special lilting accents and their impeccable Latin responses at Mass, all sharply distinctive evidence of their difference from the rest of us plebeian American-born colored people.'

Even those Catholics who were more like us exhibited differences that captured our childish imaginations. In our parish and in neighboring Holy Angels and St. Elizabeth's, there were southern Louisiana Creoles like the ones my mother had encountered in New Orleans. They too exhibited an aura of cultural "otherness" and self-determined specialness. They often had French surnames that were difficult to spell and pronounce, and they cultivated a form of speech with special rhythmic admixtures of French, Spanish, and Southern drawl. Then there were other Catholics whose backgrounds were more consonant with ours. The parents were first-wave Southern émigrés too, who had come North after World War I, ambitious to gain a foothold in middle-class urban life. For them, this translated into making choices that separated them from the remnants of plantation heritage and established them, in their own eyes, as above the regular crowd. Their boys were sought after as suitors by "good" families, and their girls were prim, proper, and admired. In all, the relatively small, select colored presence in the Catholic Church and the perceived rigor of Catholic schools were viewed as positive social currency throughout the wider colored community. Clearly, this particular brand of "otherness" was understood to be socially approved, creating for its adherents a privileged place on the colored sociocultural ladder.

As I grew up, it struck me as interesting that a far smaller proportion of whites were Catholics than we had thought. For us, whiteness and Roman Catholicism went hand-in-hand. After all, nearly all of the white people we encountered seemed to be Catholic. This is not surprising in view of the dense ethnicity of the white Roman Catholic parishes contiguous to ours. Although most of the people who owned stores on 31st and 35th Streets were Jewish, the stores around the boundaries were in Irish or Italian Catholic Bridgeport; the men who worked in the factory alongside our father were Polish Catholics; our white teachers were almost all Catholic; and the children whose teams we played against were Catholic, too. The mayor of Chicago was Catholic, as were most of the aldermen.

It seemed peculiar to learn from reading American novels such as those of F. Scott Fitzgerald and Theodore Dreiser that perceptible Roman Catholic "foreignness" might consign one to a *lower* class position than that of one's white Anglo-Saxon Protestant counterparts. It was clear to us that if this was true for *some* people, they definitely did not live in Chicago. A prominent Episcopal bishop once told a reporter that his decision to convert from Roman Catholicism to Episcopalianism was made in part because of his Irish mother's thinking that this choice accorded him increased social status and upward mobility. But he ended up in California. Not Chicago.

Both of our parents, characteristically iconoclastic, disdained social climbing, thought an emphasis on the exotic was pretentious if not silly, and judged Catholic schools somewhat precious and certainly undemocratic. Nonetheless, if their oldest daughter wanted to go that route, not for any of the nonsensical, status-seeking motivations that they disparaged, but for personal reasons that they respected—namely, love—well, that was okay.

Zoe definitely loved Pat, and thus Catholicism emerged as a positive choice for her. It must be said that the Roman Catholic Church was also a logical fit for her basic mystical predilections. The firstborn daughter, Zoe had always been our mother's closest confidante, in some ways the sister Day had yearned for, although they were really very different personalities. While our mother was a permanent pragmatist, our sister was always fascinated by the arcane. She was the first person I ever knew who was familiar with such things as auras and signs, categories that Day dismissed, but interests that she tolerated as quirks of her oldest girl.

Zoe used to entertain us by recounting the story of a local psychic, Miz Bigneck, who had been a friend of our Uncle Fred and Aunt Sarah in the old days. This odd name, assigned to her because of the hugely enlarged goiter that dominated her presence, was borne by Miz Bigneck with the unflappable equanimity of the Deep South, where people are often called by descriptive names that might in another culture seem untoward if not unkind. We had neighbors like Crazy Walter, who really did have serious mental problems, and who used to unpredictably and with no visible provocation run to one of the building's hallway windows and scream out at the top of his lungs. With the unexamined cruelty of children, we would follow him to the window, imitating his mournfully repeated, inexplicable cries: "Jo-se-phus! Jo-se-phus!!" We knew, too, Fat James, who was indeed very fat but was much admired for his intelligence, acumen, and beautifully precise speech. Then there were Mr. Hunchback down the street, and Spotty, whose face was completely covered with pockmarks. The thing was, people just took these things for granted.

Anyway, our mother disliked Miz Bigneck to begin with because she was too idle. Big, as the grownups usually called her for short, could sit around all day doing nothing but commenting on things in general. Then one day in the early fall of 1938 when our mother and Zoe were visiting Aunt Sarah, Miz Bigneck had said dryly, "So, Day, you're having another little baby." Day furiously denied that she was pregnant—she had, in fact, only come to that conclusion herself a few days before and hadn't told anybody yet. Miz Bigneck just said, "Well, Miz Day-rest, whether you want to say so or not, you're having another little girl, a red one. I see her standing right in front of you." When Audrey was born just short of nine months later, she was indeed a red one, a Southern term for the very light-skinned, had stick-straight hair and looked for all the world like a papoose, as people said. Zoe liked to tease our mother about Miz Bigneck, and Day would just tighten her lips. It was just foolishness to think people could see things that hadn't happened yet.

The Rones never took the back of anybody's hand, and Zoe

as the older sibling was definitely our role model. She once walked out on a class with Bruno Bettelheim, the famed University of Chicago psychologist, because he was rude to her. She never went back. As family archivist and historian, our oldest sister kept videotapes and scrapbooks with articles on everyone's accomplishments. She was an absolutely inveterate collector of objects from all of her family's travels to Europe and North Africa, but mostly to Mexico, to which they returned again and again. These cultural treasures filled their home, and she also took them into her classroom to share with her students and their families. She had eschewed her career as a school psychologist to work as a classroom teacher because she felt she could have more impact there in daily contact with children, and subsequently she won a citywide award for outstanding teaching.

Our children and Zoe's were always close. They shared backyard barbecues and baseball games, graduations and family gossip, and both of her boys, devoutly Catholic, brought deep joy to their parents by becoming doctors, one an obstetrician and the other a psychologist. Occasionally as a family, for whatever special reason, we went back to our old church, St. James, or to Zoe's neighborhood church, St. Dorothy's. Our parents would not accompany us. The five of us siblings would go together, and when we knelt at Mass and prayed, it felt just like the old days, when we were all just little, somehow through our oldest sister's shepherding brought into contact with something one might call the holy.

CHAPTER 16. *Naming the Holy*

The Holy is mostly about not-name.
Rivers, children, oceans, stars, stones,
encountered, met in the fleeting
      Known in the not-known.
Holy the firm, but also the not-firm
and the infirm and the impossibly
unfirmable.
Holy the not-yet
Brown husks of bulbs in nearly invisible shimmy
beneath the frozen Ground of Being
sentient with their own
inevitable and ineffable bloom.
Holy their thousand tulip colors to Be,
pale or vivid intensities of scarlet
or purple or gold

By our own Ninety-Nine Million and One names
we are called
into the Holy silence
and here tongue and there teeth
without speech
make sound
utter the falling / not-name / not-idea
Kumbayah.

· RONNE HARTFIELD

Day Shepherd had as clear and strong a faith in God as
any I have ever encountered, but hers was her own private, anom-
alous faith. She knew a lot of scriptures learned at Mamán's knee
and very occasionally would pull up one Bible verse or another

to illustrate something. She took the Bible stories with a grain of salt, though, long before all of the flap about the historical Jesus became a conversation. Bible stories were exactly that—stories—important and valuable, but she believed firmly in evolution and thought the number of years lived by the Hebraic prophets, the raising of Lazarus, and a few other things were preposterous. She taught her children the Ten Commandments and the Lord's Prayer in much the same way she taught us the Pledge of Allegiance (I always suspected that churches and governments were somewhat parallel in our mother's lexicon— they were all human constructs, open to inquiry and critique).

That notwithstanding, and whatever she made God out to be, our mother had an unquestioning belief in something one can call the sacred. We knew she prayed privately for all of us, and she had a deeper soul than many religious people in my experience. There was one family ritual that conveyed authentically some of our mother's unspoken feelings about that. Every night when she put each of us to bed—she did always come and kiss us goodnight until we moved away from home—we would say together that child's simple prayer that begins "Now I lay me down to sleep, I pray the Lord my soul to keep." She spoke those words with us in a soft, quiet voice, with her hand on our head, and what I remember always is the tenderness of those moments. I *knew* even as a small child that she wanted us to feel safe, watched over by some power larger than merely her own. As a young mother, I repeated that rite with my own little girls, aware that there was no real way I alone could keep them safe. I realized then that a prayer for safety would have been an especially deep thing for Day, who had been left without sure protection at a very young age. It set me to thinking about how much her mother's premature death had affected her beliefs, and how an inward trembling might be held at bay by a toss of the head.

Our mother's attitudes toward our religious education were, in consonance with her fundamental character, liberating and highly idiosyncratic. Since neither of our parents attended church, the oldest two children had very little experience with churches of any kind until they were old enough to manifest some religious curiosity on their own. My mother did come to church with me, and later with her grandchildren, on state occasions—baptisms; confirmations; sometimes on Mother's Day, when we wore red carnations in her honor; and always on Easter, when she found the Roman Catholic and Episcopal liturgies entirely too long, with "all that getting up and sitting down again." She *never* liked the part at the sharing of the peace where you had to shake hands with all those strangers, and after she hit her maximum with one or two Peace Be With Yous, she would just sit down, square her shoulders, and stare straight ahead.

Our mother never liked much of anything about church, actually. She was simply too individualistic, too singular, to find any strength or comfort in communal rites (except for the sacrosanct rituals of the family, but that was a different thing). She trusted *us;* she did not trust institutions that claimed to have the truth about everything, and she was wary of public demonstrations of emotion. Because of the passion of its collective expressivity, which Day thought unseemly, and its insistent emotional outpouring, which Day deemed overly fervid and perhaps overly facile, the profound treasury of black church music was largely absent from our lives. Nonetheless, living in the community, we absorbed some of it inevitably when we attended funerals and visited other people.

We had two little girl neighbors named Rosemary and Juanita whose mother had all these old seventy-eights of Mahalia Jackson gospels songs. Juanita had heard the famed Mahalia in person, she told us. She and her mother used to close their eyes and wave their hands over their heads, singing along to words like, "If I have wounded any souls today, dear Lord forgive." Unlike my mother, who accepted but could not understand this inclination in her own daughter, I was absolutely mesmerized by these songs and, as I am now, deeply stirred. My own lifelong passion for this music began way back then, and I continue to be humbled by the power of the soul-filled human voice to shatter boundaries. Songs like *Precious Lord* or *Balm in Gilead* are for me a gift, a particularly black legacy speaking a message that can sustain in the midst of sorrow, individual or communal.

When they are sung quietly and without the insistent, nearly hypnotic drama of some renditions, even Day might respond to these messages. I wish she could have drawn comfort from them. She could not, but if such expressions of worship had meaning for her children, she respected our differences. The richly varied fruits of our mother's eclectic indulgence continue to be visible in the worship life as well as in the music libraries of all her children and grandchildren. My spirit is enlarged and deepened equally by the Latin sonorities of "Adoro Te Devote" and Mozart's "Laudate Deum," and by "Fix Me, Jesus, Fix Me." Zoe's sons, Skippy and Scooter, asked that both Franck's "Panis Angelicus" and Mahalia's "If I Can Help Somebody" (". . . then my living shall not have been in vain") be sung at their mother's last rites.

When Zoe began her initial forays into Roman Catholicism, she was fourteen or fifteen years old, and the weekly drama at our local Roman Catholic church, St. James, was absolutely compelling. One should not underestimate, however, the influence of the good-looking Patterson boy across the street, whose family were devoutly practicing Catholics. All ten of the Patterson clan were regular Mass- and confession-goers, and as Zoe took her place as Pat's steady girlfriend, so did she become a devout Roman Catholic. Following her lead, so did all four of us younger Rone children. Our parents expressed little concern about this developing interest in churchgoing among their brood, but they had no intention of changing their own position on the Roman Catholics. As radical individualists, they neither understood nor trusted the idea of One True Church. Their position was that our involvement wasn't likely to hurt us; it showed respect for our oldest sister, and we would certainly learn *something*. Learning was obviously a higher value in our household than piety.

Some of us fell away after a while, mainly affronted by the nuns' over-concern about the infernal prospects awaiting our infidel mother and father, whose unmovable stance was that we could not go to a Catholic school even if scholarships were proffered. Zoe and Audrey did continue for the rest of their lives as relatively devout Roman Catholics. Audrey married a Catholic from Philadelphia and settled with him in Christ the King parish in Chicago's Beverly neighborhood, and Pat and Zoe's two sons graduated at the top of their classes at De La Salle High, where Mayor Daley's boys had gone, and where the prevailing racial prejudice only increased their determination to excel. Arthur floated around the edges of Protestantism, ultimately marrying a pretty schoolteacher from Birmingham, Alabama, whose family was so Baptist that no liquor could be served at their wedding reception. My brothers creatively arranged a second postnuptial at the local black-owned hotel, with suitable libations for a festive all-night celebration, which was attended, of course, by many happy, younger-generation Baptists.

Jay and I, the poetic ones of the family, were permanently captured by the solemnity and power of the pre–Vatican II Roman Catholic liturgy, but we ended up in the arms of the other branch of the Holy Catholic Church, what my mother called "those Episcopals" and what my teenage Catholic boyfriend called "King Henry's boys." After a mid-teenage year of exploration, I had found the sermons of Baptists and Presbyterians too long, and I thought the Lutherans too wordy altogether. I visited the Unitarians and Congregationalists with serious-minded high school friends and liked the warm welcome extended by their members, but finally the services seemed to me more like community meetings than like church.

Once I was invited to what my father called a hellfire church by a lovely quiet girl named Inez, who read a lot of books like I did and whose brother Leo was the star classical pianist of our neighborhood. Their pastor really did preach hellfire and damnation for anybody who walked away from the service *that day* without acknowledging Jesus Christ as their personal Savior. This injunction scared me half to death, because of course no Rone child would assent to something they didn't understand at all. The pastor interrogated me in a small anteroom after church, and when I continued to express my reservations and to affirm that I had to consult my parents anyway, he became increasingly annoyed. He finally dismissed me with some sort of warning that I likely had trouble ahead. When I got home and told this story over dinner more or less word-for-word—it was, after all, a small drama, the sort of thing the family loved to listen to and discuss—my parents were enraged and discouraged me from ever again visiting Inez, not to mention her church. My brother Arthur, teasing, called me Trouble Ahead for weeks. I, always overly accessible to the prophetic, could not immediately shake off my discomfort, and I looked warily over my shoulder for months before I finally got over this encounter.

There was another Christian denomination that played a large role in my life as well. We younger children had been nurtured along the way by wonderfully affirming Sunday school teachers at nearby Hartzell Methodist. The Sampson family, who were very active there, were distant relatives of my aunt Ola's first husband, the one who had joined up with Marcus Garvey's movement and gone off to Liberia. I learned to sing Handel's Messiah in the Hartzell AME Young People's Choir, which used to travel to sing around the Midwest at other black Methodist churches, and I made my first ever trip alone at age fourteen— to Beloit, Wisconsin, to visit a family I had met on one of those choir trips. We choir kids would be housed in the homes of local church people, and this particular family, who were lovely people, had taken a liking to me and invited me back to visit them that summer by myself.

I rode up to Beloit on a Greyhound bus, wearing a straw hat and white gloves. My mother had bought me a long flowered crepe nightgown to sleep in, so I felt quite grown-up—except that I was still radically flat-chested, a fact made embarrassingly clear by the sheerness of the flowered gown. I shared a bedroom with the family's green-eyed daughter, Bunny, who though exactly my age was considerably more mature, physically and socially. The kids at my urban high school were naive innocents compared to these small-town colored teens with their own cars and accompanying back-seat activity. So as I despaired over my childish body and woeful lack of sexual sophistication, my mother hushed me, saying that the reason girls like Bunny were called fast was that they were in too much of a hurry to do everything. Wasn't it clear that when you turned the fire up too fast and too high, the pot got burned and nothing inside was fit to eat? "You just take your time," she said. But this was my mother, who always listened. Before packing my suitcase, she shredded a couple of old nylon stockings and sewed them inside silken coverings to create for me a pair of little brassiere pads with snaps to fit inside the top of my gown.

I couldn't really stay with the Methodists though. Without articulation I was seeking something inchoate, something of what Emily Dickinson called that "formal feeling," and I finally found it, when I was fifteen years old, in the Anglican tradition. Jay did too, and his son, Butchie, later became an acolyte at Trinity Episcopal, just a couple of blocks away from St. James. By the time my own children came along, girls could be acolytes too, and it has been a particular joy to me to watch my daughters, and more recently my granddaughters, marching down the aisle of our neighborhood house of worship, the Episcopal Church of St. Paul and the Redeemer, proudly carrying the cross or solemnly censing the nave.

Still, the continuing influence of our parents precludes any of us from certain traditional dogmatic acceptances. They raised a tribe of what could be called, I suppose, questioning Christians. One Episcopal rector to whom I was especially close called me an expanded Christian. I look on that still as a term of endearment. I was allowed to pursue my love of black music and my undogmatic, eccentric Anglicanism in cognizance of family histories. Our father's St. Louis sister, Aunt Bessie, was a high-church Baptist who, when we visited her, would sometimes sing what she called old Louisiana songs like "Some Bright Morning When This Life Is O'er, I'll Fly Away," with the same gestures as Juanita's mother, but our father had no truck with any of it. He loved to sing, but singing, for him, was not worship. When Audrey and I came home and repeated the songs, complete with Aunt Bessie's closings of the eyes, both of our parents would roll their eyes, so we did too, even as I always harbored some serious response in my heart.

My mother intuited this and worried about it. On the one hand, she wanted to respect her children and their choices, albeit different from her own. On the other hand, somehow Emmaline and Mamán had brought her up that too much focus on church was "common," and not a *sensible* thing at all. Then, of course, there was the position of her father. Clearly his colored children could not go to the white Episcopal church attended by his mother, Miz Kate. Still, he did not want them mixed up with the colored church with all of the field hands who worked for him. I imagine at that time, in the early 1900s, that little church would have been inhabited by people only recently emerged from slavery, its rites of worship still resonant with the sounds of Africa. My mother's father would have wanted, I suspect, to keep some distance between the traditions of two truthful histories, uneasily mindful of his connection to and responsibility for the three children who bore his name and likeness.

It seems likely that the peculiar outlines of her father's role in her life contributed to Day's firm assertion that no minister or priest was "one whit" closer to the truth than anybody else. Day was reared with a multigenerational inherited history of cultural skepticism that extended itself to established religious dogmas and practices. Whose "truth," singular or collective, could, after all, create a clear logic that would explain the trajectory of her experiences? Like her father, Mama Emmaline, and Mamán before her, Day Shepherd was skeptical to the bone.

Both of our parents thought that most people, when they got into what they called "that holy-holy thing," were hypocrites. When I asked my mother what she thought about heaven and hell, her answer was characteristic: "You all just make sure that when I go I'm buried in my best underthings, not wrapped in one of those little half-to-the-waist things undertakers use. If I am going to meet my maker, I don't want to be embarrassed." In her last year, when she began to suffer a series of ministrokes, she set aside a dresser drawer for her burial underwear, ironed and sacheted, and we followed her wishes. Our mother refused to talk with us about anything one could call faith or the soul, becoming intensely uncomfortable whenever the topic emerged. "I don't even know what people mean by those kinds of words," she would say, turning away, "those are *private* things."

Predictably, she did finally tell me she thought it was okay for me to study religion. With the tender bemusement she reserved for her children, she cautioned me: "Just please don't start hanging a lot of crosses around, dahr-ling, and promise me you won't become a lady preacher. That would be one thing you could do that would be just too hard for me to understand." Fortunately, I suppose, I got the degree in theology without ever being drawn to the ministry.

Day lived long enough to sit through two of her grandchildren's weddings, Skippy's in a Roman Catholic church, Holy Angels, and Claire's in the University of Chicago's Bond Chapel. This last one was conducted by an Episcopal clergyman and family friend, who gave a beautiful homily for our eldest daughter and her groom. Before he got to the end of his remarks, Day became impatient and spoke up sharply and altogether audibly: "He's talking too *long*." She was ready to see the bride and groom kiss and proceed down the aisle. The rest was extra. Formal ceremony was just never the way Day Shepherd thought people should take up time in the world.

CHAPTER 17. *Strange Fruit*

Strange fruit hanging from the Southern trees
Black bodies swinging in the southern breeze

· BILLIE HOLIDAY

In the middle of our mother's adult life, little Emmett Till was murdered. Barely fourteen years old, he was still teetering on the precipice of adolescence. And it was that chubby, big-eyed brown boy from the South Side of Chicago who was beaten without mercy and thrown into a ditch down in Money, Mississippi, on the outskirts of Greenwood. Little Emmett Till was lynched just as that word was fading from our memory. Lynched in the most fearsome manner, just like old-time Negroes used to tell stories about. For flirting, "taking liberties," with a young white woman, is what the newspapers said.

When it happened in the summer of 1955 I was nineteen years old, and I had known Emmett. His family lived almost next door to my aunt Nettie, one of the Lehmann cousins, and her husband, my uncle Bennie Ransom, had watched over him along with our rambunctious cousin Junior, who had been a constant playmate of Emmett's. They were two of a kind, those boys. Those who knew him well believed the story that Emmett had whistled at a white girl. Why not? Emmett was saucy, insouciant, what we called, with a twinkle, "mannish." He had the kind of audacity people like us applauded. What Emmett's mother said was that she had *taught* her son to whistle as a means of coping with his stammering problem—when he couldn't form a consonant, he would whistle. What none of us realized was that the rules in the South hadn't changed as much as anybody thought, and those rules still did not allow for audacity in a black boy. Especially when it came to whistling—whether intentional or not—near a white woman.

Things had been in an uproar since Thurgood Marshall's 1954 victory in *Brown v. Board of Education*. Indeed a thin thread of "What will they do now?" anxiety lurked beneath the triumph felt in communities of color when the seminal Supreme Court decision came down, ordering the desegregation of all schools in this country, those in Mississippi included. People wondered whether the astonished white population of the South would do something crazy in retaliation or just sit it out and hope that what they characterized as an outrage would somehow go away.

But for the people in our neighborhood on the South Side of Chicago, the murder of little Louis Emmett Till was not simply about civil rights or desegregation or anybody's court case. This was personal. This was a little black boy whose hard-working parents had made a home in a nice neighborhood in the North. They had left behind night riders and Jim Crow, but they sent their children Down Home every summer just like everybody did, to be coddled by grandparents and praised by extended family, and to keep in touch with the old, nurturing ways. Just like everybody. This is why the terrible newspaper and television images of Emmett's bloated, massacred little body sent shock waves through all of our homes and churches, and why the massive response that ensued sent so many thousands to the funeral home and to their own neighborhood churches to grieve and to rage. My mother said flatly that we all had a part in it because as colored people we had let Emmett down, because we hadn't cautioned him or counseled him, because we had nearly forgotten the dark terrors of the South we had left behind.

People, especially the young, spoke of a possible riot, and workplaces where black and white worked side by side pretty comfortably grew tense and silent—it was understood that the least wrong word could inflame somebody. My own white friends were social and political liberals, and they joined us in anger, deploring what had happened, but the horror and pain suffered by people of color was different—Emmett's murder was rooted in collective memory. It was Billie Holiday's "strange fruit," it was the Scottsboro Boys, it was lived stories choked at the backs of the throats of men like my own father. Dray Rone had fled Louisiana in dread of what the persistent and unwanted affections of a local white girl might bring down upon him. It was all of this darkness and all of this helpless terror to be lived out yet again.

Those with deep remembrance just shook their heads and said, "Uh-huh." Too many people had lulled themselves into thinking such things would never happen again. I had just graduated from the University of Chicago and was working downtown in a sophisticated publishing company. Like many young black college graduates of my time, I had thought myself en route to an enlightened, color-free existence. Emmett's murder changed that. My parents and their friends spoke of little else for weeks. Gradually, though, even that atrocity receded from kitchen-table conversation, because by the end of the year all talk was now riveted on Montgomery, Alabama.

Just before the year was out, Mrs. Rosa Parks, a dignified colored lady in that profoundly segregated city, refused to give up her bus seat to a white man, igniting more than a decade of radical change. Something called the civil rights movement was formally begun, and it swept through the nation, with Chicago in its wake. Our mother and father were puzzled by the growing unrest among what they still called colored people. They admired Dr. Martin Luther King Jr. because of the brilliance of his speech, both formal and informal, and because of what conveyed itself as true conviction, an encomium reserved for only a few in Day's world. Malcolm X's obvious thoughtful, informed intelligence impressed them as well. They were the kind of people who thought Islam, no matter what brand, a profoundly foreign construct, but even the televised sit-ins and marches and the huge church-based protests were startlingly new to their thinking.

These were people who had been raised to pursue their own path and to take care of their family, not to join mass movements. The civil rights movement attracted so many people of all ages and colors, who found hope, meaning, and power in binding their individual lives to the group struggle, but Day could never sway with the prevailing winds of collective possibility. She harbored a fundamental distrust that her individual interests would be clearly perceived, not to mention well served, by any group. This was the same woman who had trusted her intuitive thinking enough to marry the man she loved, contravening the advice and judgment of even her closest family. As well, this was the same woman whose father had obstinately created another way home for his colored family, in opposition to his mother's will and to the mores of his community. Day Shepherd Rone was a radical individualist by heritage as well as inclination.

Television brought the change right into all of our homes, and for perhaps the first time in their experience, our parents had to rely on their children to help make sense of the world, rather than vice versa. The slogans of Black Power that later swept through the land seemed radically unrealistic to these Southerners, who only knew the path of gradual improvement of one's lot by means of private endeavor. They had never made the linguistic and political transition from the descriptive term *colored* to *Negro*, and they never did make the term *black* a part of their lexicon. Over many evenings we talked about this new world, building bridges with articles and books. Still, our mother and father remained permanently uncertain about activism as a strategy for freedom or dignity.

In the 1960s Chicago was one of the nation's most kinetic hubs of civil rights activity, arguably the single most important Northern center. Dr. King was in and out of the city regularly until he finally moved his family here in the middle of the decade. Ralph Abernathy, who was to be Dr. King's successor as the head of the Southern Christian Leadership Conference (SCLC), came here for strategy meetings, as did Southern leaders like Andrew Young, C. T. Vivian, Jim Bevel, Ed Riddick, and others. I met many of these intense, impassioned young ministers on one occasion or another and was mesmerized by the power of their conviction. Northern activists with names that were to become legendary, Jesse Jackson, Al Raby, and Dick Gregory, were critical in breaking through the stony walls of corporate resistance to affirmative action, in forcing improvements in school conditions, and in demanding new jobs and contracts for black workers. They organized citizens' associations such as Operation Push and Operation Breadbasket, and held strategy sessions at the Urban Training Center led by charismatic Episcopal priest James Morton, who later called many of these leaders to the pulpit at Manhattan's Cathedral of St. John. Their calls for justice attracted other white civil rights workers, too, including Roman Catholic priests like Father Groppi from Milwaukee and antiwar activists like the Berrigan brothers from New York City.

Young people I knew were swept along by the brilliant, dedicated dynamism of these leaders, who convinced us that we could—and would—change our world. Here they all were, gathered right here in Chicago to crystallize what had come to be called simply the Movement. Our parents listened with interest to our recountings of what was happening in their city, but they never came to share our sense of the Movement's promise.

Any incipient empathies Day might have had concerning the civil rights movement were brought to an end by two traumatic events, one public and one private. First, in 1963 President John F. Kennedy was shot dead. He was the public figure who had helped to bridge the old world she had understood and this confusing new one with its organizing and marching and all those people singing out in the streets. Jack Kennedy was the first American president she had felt any connection to since FDR, and she thought he had some backbone. He had spoken out for civil rights, as had his spunky younger brother, whom she, like everyone else, called Bobby. She liked the Kennedy mystique, liked it that this president was a young man with a young family, and television images of his little son playing under his desk made her smile. Jack Kennedy had spoken out for many things she believed in, and then he got shot in the head, right there in Dallas, Texas, that city of rednecks, while he was riding in the parade car with his young wife sitting right next to him. The nation grieved, of course, but for Day the assassination had a personal weight to it. She sensed a connection between the events preceding Kennedy's murder, with all of the marching and the singing, and the events in Dallas. To her way of thinking, if the whole country hadn't been in so much disorder, the assassination would not have happened. Her political understandings were naive, but she believed firmly that chaos breeds chaos.

Then early the next year the order she worked so desperately to maintain within her private world was profoundly threatened. Our father was frighteningly sick with cancer. He had still been strong at sixty-four, still a tease—he liked to call our mother Molly after Fibber McGee's nagging wife in the radio program—and his slow dying left Day without an echoing voice to mirror her confusion over all of this newness, without a partner who would remember with her the way things used to be. Her children had embraced this changing world to which she would never find a key. Our mother had watched the television images of Bull Connor's dogs and covered her eyes as fire hoses propelled black bodies into the air. In 1964, when the four little girls died in the bombing of their Birmingham Sunday school, our mother thought barbarism in this land had gone as low as it could go. She couldn't understand why people couldn't just *stop* all the craziness that had brought things to a point none of us could believe. The right to vote, the right to go to unsegregated schools, the opportunity for better jobs, none of it was worth the lives of little children. She determined to stop looking at the television news.

As our father's life drained away, she was left with too many memories of days that for a long time had made some kind of sense, with leftover life to find a way through by herself, and this thing called the Movement seemed to be moving the whole world except for her. Ultimately she would settle herself with the changes, as she had managed to do in other times, but she was never to overcome the feelings of alienation and estrangement from those issues that were now a national obsession.

CHAPTER 18. *Our Father's Freight Train Blues*

My father planted wells
in voices of history.
Rows of blues . . .
tangled in my weeks . . .
years in silence . . . I ritualize.

· STERLING PLUMPP

It was in early 1964 that our father was diagnosed with prostate cancer. As far as I know, the word *cancer* was never explicitly employed in his presence. His doctors, first at Michael Reese and then, when the medical insurance ran out, at Cook County Hospital, spoke of his condition as "prostate trouble," and the family followed suit. He never asked direct questions about what was wrong with him. Having been something of a hypochondriac all of his life, he was always on relatively easy terms with a wide variety of ailments.

When we were growing up, our father was said to have heart trouble, and it kept him out of work for months one year when I was just about three years old. He had to change his drinking habits that year, too. Surprisingly I remember this time clearly. My mother, pregnant with Audrey, took a day job, and I was left to my father's care. He cooked wonderful meals for the family, and he patiently taught me to tie my shoes, no small feat with my lack of manual dexterity. He also taught me to tell time, sitting me on his lap and patiently explaining how the city day was divided up into hours and minutes by the way the world moved around the sun. Down in Louisiana, he said, nobody really cared about whether it was three o'clock or six o'clock. People spoke only of sunup, midday and sunset. Of course, everyone knew the sun didn't *really* rise and set, but since that was what it *felt* like, and nobody had any words to talk with other than what it felt like, they used the old words that made sense before people knew any different. But up here in Chicago, you had to know exactly what *time* it was to go to work and get to school, and being on time was important, so I had to learn how clocks worked. I remember other things from those months too. Once I was sick and soiled my pajamas, and I cried for a long time. That was my first feeling of shame, and my father bathed me and made it all okay.

Our father often sang in the house, mornings mostly, but sometimes evenings, too, in a beautiful tenor voice I can still hear when I close my eyes. He sang all kinds of songs, country songs and city songs, and I remember some of them, having committed them to memory at that early age and on into the next many years. I would sit on top of our big steamer trunk watching him as he shaved and then slapped Mennen's aftershave lotion on first one cheek and then the other. His early morning ablutions included wet-combing his carefully barbered wiry hair and setting it in place for the day by covering it with a funny sort of cap made of an old nylon stocking, which he would remove at the last minute before he walked out the door.

Dray Rone really loved to sing. His eyes would twinkle back at me as he sang the words to "Freight Train Blues":

> You can have your blondes and your brunettes too, but
> When it comes to my gal neither one will do—
> They put on their paints and powders and look mighty fine
> But it takes a brown-skinned gal to satisfy my mind.

The words to one frequently sung lament, "What can I say dear after I say I'm sorry? What can I do to prove it to you that I'm

sorry?" always caused my mother to laugh and pick up a newspaper and throw it at him. We were never to learn what deed
had conjured up the song yet one more time, but we recognized
it as a code between them, and something warm surrounded us
when he sang it.

No doubt John Rone was something of a rogue. Neither a gam-
bler nor a womanizer, as far as we knew, he sometimes stayed
out too late on a Saturday night and came home three sheets to
the wind (an expression he hated). "A man has a right to have a
drink with friends on a weekend," he would say, "and I can hold
my liquor." He couldn't. He would start to stammer and walk
unsteadily after two shots of Old Forrester. Laughing with us
over our mother's impatience with those late nights, he said
he would put his key in the lock and throw his hat inside. If it
didn't come back at him, he knew he was okay.

Our father's singing could deteriorate into the maudlin on
those occasions when he drank too much bourbon, much to the
distress of our mother. This trait was particularly troubling on
holidays. Always observant, I learned to trace the exact trajectory of these bourbon moods. My father would go from sweet
singer to overly sentimental and sometimes teary-eyed poet
to defensive and belligerent authority-in-all-things. Like my
mother, I could manage the swift changes in demeanor with rea-
sonable patience and agility. But my sister Audrey, who from
childhood forward had no taste for the unpredictable, developed
a disinclination for our large, chaotic family celebrations that
she has never completely lost. Still, like all of us, she treasures
the memories of the singing, and we still embrace around holiday tables and, without bourbon, sing together the same old
Rone songs.

In those last months of our father's life, before he became too
weak, I would ask him to sing for me, and from time to time I
would join in and we would both sing for my girls. We spent a
lot of time together then, as he had offered to paint our entire
eight-room apartment as a gift. I felt sure that he knew he was
dying, because he had decided to do one big favor for each of us

children that year. He said it was because he was retired and had too much time on his hands. With three small girls and a new baby, I was around the house a lot, and of course, I would try to get him to tell stories. Sometimes he would, but mostly he liked to paint in quiet or sing.

Near the end our father was in a good deal of pain, so his passing was not as difficult for us as it might have been. He had to have morphine administered frequently, but in between times he still never spoke of dying. A bit more ruminative as he waned, but no less high-spirited, he would tease us that our six-year-old daughter, Claire, didn't like the life-size doll he had bought her for her birthday. "That gal's got more than a little Louisiana Choctaw in her—she thinks that big old doll has a *spirit* in it." He would laugh and laugh. He often slept on the couch, fitful in his pain and not wanting to disturb our mother. He teased her that she must be missing having her back rubbed, and in the evenings he loosened her crown of braids and brushed her still waist-length hair.

He made his sixty-fifth birthday on June 9, our parents' forty-first wedding anniversary. In July he was hospitalized. We went to see him regularly. Once, when I stopped on the way and bought lunch to take to the hospital, hamburgers and coleslaw, he chided me for bringing restaurant food, so the next day I cooked a beef stew until the meat was so tender it fell off the bones, which mollified him. Day hated going to the hospital and rationed her time there. She couldn't sleep all night after a visit. "I can't watch him waste away like that," she said, and she mostly sent meals to him by us children. She was hardening herself to his imminent death, growing a carapace. When she did go to see him, she usually went with Aunt Ola, who could talk her way through anything, and they would reminisce about the old days. When I went, Day baby-sat. "This is something I can do," she said.

Zoe and I, who were both not working at the time, drove to the hospital nearly every day, and our father loved our company. He wanted us to share all the news about Dr. King, who was organizing civil rights protests in Chicago, and he wanted to know whether we thought the Chicago police would forcibly break up the marches. He also wanted to know the news about Chicago's mob. More mob leaders were being indicted every week, it seemed, and even Momo Giancana had gone to jail. Our father had known the Al Capone days, and he still thought the mob was invincible. He thought the labor unions were invincible too, but when Jimmy Hoffa was indicted he said "That's the end of the working man. You wait and see."

We got the telephone call in the early morning of August 6 saying that our father had died. It seemed so strange that this voluble man who had always bloomed in the company of people, and especially that of his children and grands, had died alone in a hospital bed. Of course he was not really alone because all of the nurses, doctors, and nurses' aides on the floor had come to be very fond of him. Many of my neighbors, too, had gotten to know our father during those months he was painting our apartment. He had particularly enjoyed one of them, Chris Smith, who was a dean at the University of Chicago and also an ordained minister. Chris was a Southerner whose sister was married to the comedian and social activist Dick Gregory. He and Dray Rone had laughed a lot as they talked Northern politics and Down Home recollection across the back porches. Chris generously agreed to conduct the funeral services. He thickened out a relatively slight acquaintance by visiting every single member of the family, then gave a warm, rich homily, dignified but intimate, exactly right for John Drayton Rone. When Chris himself died only a few years later, I wept, remembering those shared times.

One month after our father was buried, Day cut her hair to just below her ears, the way she had worn it when she met Dray Rone. She never grew it long again.

CHAPTER 19. *Lifelines*

If I could only remember
The word, if I could make it with my breath
It would be with me forever as it was
. . . and time and the things of falling
Would not fall into emptiness but into
The light, and the word tell the way of their falling
Into the light forever, if I could remember
      And make the word with my breath.

· W. S. MERWIN

Throw out the Lifeline
Throw out the Lifeline
Someone is drowning today

· OLD NEGRO SPIRITUAL

Flowers were everywhere. The air in the house was heavy with their various cloying fragrances. "Get rid of the flowers," she said. "Throw them out. What good are they?" There it was. Nothing was any good. She could not go and look upon her son's body. In those dark days after Jay died, when we walked dazed through the necessary rituals, choosing a coffin, seeing to an Episcopal ceremony and newspaper death notices, our mother would not, could not be moved away from her rocking chair at home, where she sat, stilled, eyes too terrible for us to bear. Her grief was monumental, mythic, without hope of remedy. At a different moment in a different place, her keening might have reached toward heaven. Here, only silence.

Arthur and Audrey had flown down South to get me. I had taken the City of New Orleans *Down Home to visit my brother Ben, who was seriously ailing, and they couldn't tell this thing to me over the phone, this news that a massive heart attack had ended the life of my firstborn son. They couldn't say the words, but when I awoke that morning to find them at my bedside with their faces all destroyed, I sat up in that bed because I knew something had happened. Then, "Somebody is hurt," I said. They told me later that the words I spoke could barely break through on my tongue. "No. Somebody is dead. It's Jay isn't it?" I collapsed, right then. It was November 1968. The year of all those assassinations. Dr. Martin Luther King Jr. had been gunned down in April at the age of thirty-nine, and now my son, the same age. Gone.*

Dr. King and our brother Jay had been born only a few weeks apart, and though the trajectories of their lives had been very different, they shared some fundamental qualities: an easy charm that drew men and women to them in every situation, a passionate commitment to family and to whatever they deemed to be right, and some deep interior gravity that bordered on unnameable sadness.

Then Robert Kennedy, who had marched with Dr. King and grieved at his funeral, was murdered that year too, in his prime at the age of forty-three. The earlier deaths of the two older Kennedy brothers had left Bobby as the tough-minded standard-bearer for a family especially well-loved by black people, the last present hope for a nation wounded at the core. When Bobby was gunned down, the television cameras showed his suddenly small fallen body being tended by his close friend, the famed black football star Rosey Grier. While the nation mourned once again, black Americans just about gave up any hope for real change in this country. We were a people in grief. These many deaths. These beautiful young men. And these families left with air on their tongues and lifelines to weave.

At the funeral services, I sat in the front pew with my children. I had my eyes open, but I couldn't see a thing. I felt like the bones of a dead bird, all crushed, covered all in black. So many mourners. The room could not contain all of them, or all of the grief that swelled through and around us in that room. There were lines of people, four deep, all the way to the corner, men with their hats in their hands, women from the old neighborhood sharing our sorrow.

Images washed through me, imaginings conjured up without my willing them. My firstborn son. An entirely beautiful boy, with bones and features so delicate we couldn't trace where they came from. He had to be named, of course, after his father, but he was recognized as mine from the beginning, Jay, his mother's own. Our second son three years later was named for my father, but he was so like your father and was understood from the start to be his daddy's boy.

My two boys were always close, the one protecting the other in every situation. I picture the two of them, always side by side, laughing or clowning around in their goofy boyish way. Jay I picture as a little boy, always with the most serious eyes, always teaching the younger ones. Later, in high school, Jay worked at Sealtest Ice Cream for a while, and that summer we had ice cream treats every day for dessert. His boss liked him, like everybody did, and was generous with him.

All through school, his teachers loved him too. He had old-fashioned courtly manners, and he always did his homework so careful. The younger children begged him to write out and recite his stories and poems for them. Mostly they were just gamemaking, comic things about the family and everybody we knew. I never remember his saying no.

Jay played the saxophone, and his friend Harold McGee played the drums. I loved McGee, too. He was such a formal young man, and he always wore a shirt and tie beneath his sweater. McGee and Jay and these friends of theirs would come over and play this music they called be-bop. All they could talk about was music people, Prez and Hamp and Sarah and Ella. They were so kind to you younger children, and they always let you sit around on the floor like an audience when they practiced.

Jay had a girlfriend. Her name was Minette, and she was such a nice, pretty girl, tall and slender, with long hair. She was quiet and shy, even more than he was, and she wore white dresses. But the other girl was freer *and faster, and she set her cap for him, and she won, pregnant with his child at age sixteen. He was always responsible and married her against everybody's advice. Shepherd stubbornness. I took all three of them in and helped to raise the baby, Butchie, who after all that was the sunshine of our lives. He was the best baby, smart as a whip, and talking before he was two, saying everything he wanted to.*

When your brother Arthur was hospitalized so early in his own marriage, Jay helped to pay the rent on their new apartment in Lake Meadows so he could keep it for the new wife and baby to come. Jay was a present-giver, so free-handed you just had to stop him. If you just said you liked something, he would bring it home from the store the next day. I complained one time too many about my old ice box, and he had me a new Frigidaire delivered to the house, the top of the line. He would buy me a new pocketbook if I saw somebody with one and admired it. He bought me the first electric cake mixer I ever had, and the first blender, and a brand-new waffle iron that made two waffles at a time instead of one. He sometimes would surprise you with something, like the time he brought me home a ruby ring in a velvet box. It would never have entered my mind to want a ruby ring, but it was my birthstone, and he saw it in a window downtown and decided I had to have it. I used to wear it when I went out special. Now I never take it off.

He always bought those fancy silk stockings for Zoe, the kind she likes, and at Christmas he was Santa Claus and got Audrey a Sparkle Plenty doll, the one from that comic strip, and a suitcase full of clothes for her.

Most of the important presents of my own early life were entirely unanticipated gifts from Jay. He was a seer who saw just what you needed to have. When I was about seven years old and beginning piano lessons, I wanted desperately to have my own piano, a practical impossibility in our crowded space. Jay brought home a miniature piano so I could practice in our apartment instead of always seeking out a friendly neighbor amenable to incessant scales. For my tenth Christmas he bought me a shiny red suitcase filled with a dozen children's classics with bright red covers, and a stamp so I could put my name inside each book. When I graduated from eighth grade, Jay bought me a Benrus rose-gold wristwatch. When I graduated from high school, he bought me a Smith Corona portable typewriter and a five-piece matched set of Samsonite luggage, things *Seventeen* magazine said a girl should have when going off to college—no matter that the University of Chicago dormitory was only a few blocks down the street from home.

When I earned my B.A., I had my eye on an unapproachably expensive cardigan coat, the color of the underside of oak leaves, that hung in the window of Russeks on North Michigan Avenue. I am wearing it, his gift, in some of the graduation photos, the warmth of that June day notwithstanding. Our mother is there too in the snapshots, wearing the white short coat she used to call her chubby, and her white hat with a feather. She has a cane, having broken her hip the winter before. Also there with us was Gail Westgate, my college roommate, a lifetime friend much loved by all of our family. The fact that Gail was a white Lutheran girl from the northern suburbs of Chicago, a doctor's daughter, had never been significant for any of us. What mattered was what we shared: a profound love of art and books and flowers, an endless curiosity and humor about the given world, a respect for the unknowable, and a rich connection to our families. Because Gail was so close to us all, she suffered this death with us too, knowing the unbearable weight of it for our mother.

Some central meaning of our mother's life, and of whatever it was that defined our core family, did indeed die with Jay. Day was fundamentally a mother, and that mother's strength had woven the ropes of steel flesh that gave us our strength. Her swift sweetness was the nucleus of our confidence, her wise counsel the marrow of our collective consciousness. And she couldn't save him. Nor could we. She had always taught us that we five children were like five fingers on one hand. She would hold one of our hands in hers and show us how if one finger wasn't working, then the whole system was disabled. Now, with only the remnant four, in grief without end, we set as our task the saving of our mother.

She wept in silence and from some unstoppable source. Her

body refused nourishment and we watched helplessly as her flesh fell away from wasted muscle and light departed from her face. She lost over one-third of the weight of her always slender body. When we grasped her hand, it was feverish and dry, nearly weightless; only the persistence of her bones was left to be fiercely cradled in the hands of her children. The term *flesh of my flesh* now escaped cliché.

For the length of fourteen months, Day's children took turns at her side, our collective will focused like a laser on restoring light to her eyes. I saw my own four little girls off to their schools and then drove straight to our mother to sit again in that still apartment. Zoe would come every day at three when her schoolteacher duties were ended and stay until Audrey came home from her downtown executive job. Arthur brought breakfast every day and made coffee, having made arrangements with his hospital lab that he could come late. We all took turns on weekends, bringing traditional delicacies—black walnut ice cream, cheddar cheese, and ginger snaps, potato salad with peppers, ham sandwiches—anything to tempt her to eat a little. We could occasionally get her to eat a few bits of something, but we couldn't get her to talk. After a few months, she would occasionally let us take her out to her places, Denny's, the Pancake House, Mister Stephen's, in the old neighborhood by Michael Reese. Sometimes on the way there she would cover her face and begin a deep weeping, and we would turn the car around and drive her back home again.

Our mother was drowning. That was as plain as day. And our tribe, diminished as we were, wove ourselves together as a rope, finally to bring her to shore. That fearful year extended through the spring of 1970, when gradually Day began to eat normally again, although she never fully recovered her weight or the indomitable resilience of her spirit. She renewed her interest in gardening, but any yellow flower could cause her to turn away, to disappear inside herself. The reason was this: on the day before Jay's funeral, we had all gathered at Zoe and Pat's house, exhausted and drained. At one point Zoe put down her coffee cup

with a sudden sharp movement, saying, "I can't stand the close-
ness in here—I have to get some air." Throwing a shawl about
herself, she rushed out her back door into their small yard. We
thought we'd let her have some time alone to herself, but in
about five minutes she came back into the living room in tears,
bearing armsful of tightly furled yellow roses. The backyard
rosebush, barren the day before, had unanticipatedly bloomed.
In late November. In Chicago.

CHAPTER 20. *Last Years*

❧❧

> I can hear the sound of much emptiness now. A shift of my head
> this way to the right, that way to the left. . . . It holds no fear,
> only a growing curiosity. I only wish to know it so that I may one
> day tell myself the story of my existence within it.
>
> · JAMAICA KINCAID

I always thought I'd go back Down Home. For a long time I couldn't imagine growing old in Chicago. After I moved over here to Beverly to help your sister out, I realized that whether I had planned it or not, Chicago was the end of the line for me. It just crept up on me that I was never going to move back. Nearly everybody I knew Down Home is gone, died, or moved away anyway. Just a few cousins left. And all my children up here, and all these years I got used to the city. I'm not really sure how I got used to it, but it was gradual, and when I go back home now, I feel like a visitor.

What is strange is that sometimes I feel like a visitor out here too. The streets over here in Audrey's neighborhood look pretty, but they are so empty of people you know except when I go to the Jewel. There I know all the checkout girls, and the man who helps bag the vegetables and fruit is always friendly — we joke around about how he can tell I'm a country woman because I know how to test when a melon or a tomato is not ripe no matter how good it may look. *I like to pick out my own fresh pro-*

*duce—and my own meat. I just can't trust Audrey or Tony or any of
you to select for me. You all are not strict enough with the store people.*

*I appreciate it that you drive me over to the Jewel, but one of the
things I miss the most is walking to the store on my own. That's another
thing I don't like about this neighborhood—nothing is near enough to
walk to. Remember when we had Mr. Ross' store across the street, and
nobody ever had to worry about running out of anything? He was not a
smiling man, Mr. Ross, but he had respect for people. It's hard for people
around here to have* respect*—maybe because you don't see each other
regular. I think it's better to see people in a lot of different circumstances.
That way you learn something about each other. The way it is out here,
you just maybe nod and say hello. That's all.*

When she was just short of eighty years old, we persuaded
our mother to move in with Audrey and Tony. What we told
her was that they needed her help. They both worked at demanding jobs, and their little daughter, Jennie, had to be seen
off to private school early mornings, to be delivered again by
the school bus at the end of the afternoon. The baby, Michael,
needed to be bundled up and taken to Day's house before eight
o'clock each morning, sometimes half asleep. If Day could move
in with them, it would solve a lot of cumbersome logistical problems for Audrey's little family and provide regularity and security for the children.

The underlying reason was a much more worrisome security
issue. Our fears for our mother's safety were growing each year.
Her nice Chatham apartment building with its caring, watchful
neighbors had proved to be vulnerable to new crime waves. Occasional break-ins and muggings of elderly people were reported
on her very block, producing gnawing anxieties and sleepless
nights for all of us. We worried that Day's indomitable, feisty
nature might result in physical injury to her increasingly frail
little person. She had an unrealistic picture of her ability to pro-
tect herself—and even us, if we needed it. After all, she had
long since committed herself to a rigorous exercise regimen and
could touch her toes without bending her knees, a feat that none

of her children could accomplish. So we had to make a persuasive case, and she ultimately agreed to give up her own place and move miles southwest to occupy for the last decade of her life a bedroom/sitting room on the second floor of her youngest daughter's house.

The sunny, spacious room with its own bath and an outside deck over the garden became her cosmos, and Operation Central for the family. She filled it with her familiar things, installing her own walnut bedroom set. Framed photographs of all five of her children crowded her dresser top, including several embarrassing old photos of us with former boyfriends or girlfriends. Day refused to put those photos away. "I *liked* that boy," she would say. "I don't care whether your husband likes him or not. He doesn't have to look at that picture. It's mine." Her cedar box of treasures was filled with old lockets, birth and marriage certificates, and medals won by one or another of us for swimming meets or spelling bees, or for earning membership in our high school honor society. "All of my children were smart," she would say, "smarter than the ones you picked out to marry. But that's your business."

There was an alcove for her sewing machines, the still-functioning old Singer treadle that had belonged to Mamán and the newer electric portable that one of the children had insisted she have, and on which she still did all of the family alterations. Her old oak rocker was here, too, with its brightly colored afghan once crocheted for her by Zoe when she was deep into one of her needlework periods. Tony bought a large-screen television set and installed it so Day could watch from her bed, but she never had much interest in TV except for the news and a couple of soap operas that she watched avidly. Characters from *As The World Turns* and *All My Children* took on life and breath in Day's conversation, and she would muse over their untoward deeds with the same mixture of tender forgiveness and gossipy "Do you know what that woman is doing *now?*" with which she greeted the shared stories of our friends' missteps.

All of our friends loved to visit Day, and they came often—

Arthur's medical people from the hospital; Zoe's teacher colleagues; Audrey's smart new professionals from her prolific social groups; and my friends, mostly young mothers with many small noisy children who were allowed to choose treats from Day's jars of peppermints and orange slices. Our mother's world became largely boundaried by the lives of her children and grandchildren. Not a day passed when she didn't talk to each of us, either in person or on the telephone. Since she didn't hear well, we all had to talk loudly to her, but that never seemed to hamper our conversation. Each of us knew just about everything that happened in all of our lives, except when one of us asked our mother to keep a secret, which she did, unfailingly. The smallest detail of one of the grandchildren's school grades or news of new eyeglasses threaded its way through the family, but a marital problem or emotional crisis was strictly between you and her. In the spring she gardened in Audrey and Tony's yard, producing huge, lush peonies. She sewed a little, cleaned and cooked a little, and read a little, enjoying the heat of breathless Gothic romances well into her eighties.

Until her last breath she lavished daily care on Jennie and Mike, her last two grandchildren. She actually taught Jennie to read before she entered the first grade, using the *Chicago Sun-Times* TV schedule as a textbook. The older grands came often, bringing snacks or flowery treats along with tales of their lives—details on medical school or law school exams or the special boys and girls they were courting—seeking her approval. Her old-fashioned and rigid double standard made itself vivid in these conversations—she encouraged her grandsons to "try out the girls" but continually admonished her granddaughters to maintain a clear, unchanging posture about pursuing boys: "Eyes on and hands off." Day's ethic was simple and basic: it is the female of the species who gets pregnant, contemporary availability of birth control pills notwithstanding, and pregnancy can change a girl's life permanently, no matter what one decides to do about it. Everyone of the younger generation respected her country woman's wisdom. They adored her. They endured her stories, her sharp questioning, and her imprecations, and they were soul-fed by her laughter and by the permanent availability of her profound attention to whatever was happening with and for them.

Not all of Day's visitors took equally kindly to her increasingly uncensored candor. She would suddenly and unexpectedly reveal a long-held family secret during a cousin's visit or remind one of our friends of some youthful indiscretion that no one wanted to hear about ever again. We all became very skilled at shifting such conversations, but sometimes Day would say sharply, "now stop trying to change the subject. This is interesting," and continue firmly to open whatever wounds were under the microscope at the time.

Her brood took turns taking her out for lunch or dinner and driving her to Michael Reese Hospital for her regular checkups (these visits increased incrementally as she grew older). Her doctor there grew old along with her, and what a deep pleasure it was to watch the communication between these two octogenarians, Day detailing each small symptom, her old Jewish doctor, his own eyesight and hearing diminishing, listening patiently and encouraging her to chat. Mostly she felt well, gallbladder surgeries, a broken hip, and a calcified lung from childhood notwithstanding.

Then one morning Day lost her balance while walking too briskly up Zoe's stone steps and fell backward, breaking another hip, and this time a collarbone too. She also hit her head, hard, and though she didn't have a concussion, she was eighty-four years old, and the trauma of the fall was too much to sustain. She recovered only very slowly, and we grew frightened as her inner and outer strength declined perceptibly. We decided to bring in a day-care nurse. Day was as sharp mentally as ever and wouldn't put up with the first three or four applicants. They were too proper, Day said, or too serious, or too bossy, or too churchy. One of them beat around the bush about the color thing and finally came right out and asked Audrey if our mother was "really a person of color or is she perhaps of the Caucasian persuasion?"

We were getting discouraged about the possibility of ever finding a suitable person when we were blessed with Dorothy, a large, strong, preternaturally efficient middle-aged woman whose straight-at-you competency laced with humor and deep caring equaled Day's own. Theirs was a love-at-first-sight pairing, enduring until the end. Dorothy started out coming at eight in the morning when Audrey left for work. But our mother liked company with her seven o'clock coffee, and Audrey was getting in to work later and later. So Dorothy began to come in at seven and sit with Day while they both had coffee. Dorothy had a husband who was a piece of work, they agreed, and so they would spend the first hour talking about men. Dorothy got her head so filled with stories about Dray Rone that she would repeat them to us when we came by, saying "your father was definitely a *trip*. I wish I had known him." She and Day talked about the news, and about how people take too much medicine for their own good, and agreed that there is a real difference between people who drink coffee and those who like tea. When Day decided to show her the pink silk suit and pink under things she had set aside for her burial, Dorothy said "These things are just right. You'll look real nice, Miz Rone. Real nice."

Then ensued months, nearly a year, of intermittent small strokes, followed by wild ambulance rides to the hospital and weeks of not-quite-recovery. Day was increasingly weakened and sobered each time. Though her resilience, both physical and spiritual, was amazing, it began to be apparent that she was preparing herself to die. Her stories took on a new seriousness as we stored up the lessons that would become legends. Each of us acknowledged the utter preciousness of these months, and sometimes after leaving her I would weep in the privacy of my car. The largest force in my life was diminishing, and all I could do was hold her hand.

What I never realized until a few years ago, well after our mother had died, was the *meaning* of her giving up her own place and saying goodbye to nearly all of the things that had surrounded her and given shape and continuity to her world. I had never realized the meaning of her stubborn insistence on having her own shelf in her daughter's refrigerator and in her daughter's cupboards, on eating and serving her company from her own old blue-willow plates. I had never realized what a huge transition it must have been to give away most of her own things to children and grandchildren and cousins, to give away her history and move away from her own house to that of another woman, albeit her daughter. The last change of her life. I had never realized it because she handled it with such grace. The move was *necessary*, and she was not one to lament what had to be. As always, she toughed it out, and if there were regrets, they were not spoken.

CHAPTER 21. *Omega*

We are Prisoners of our generation.

· CYNTHIA OZICK

The world will end when we forget.

· CHARLES SWINBURNE

I was driving north from my home near the University of Chicago to Mercy Hospital, where our mother lay dying. I was alone in my small red French car, which wove through the old neighborhood, nosing its way on the radar of memory around known corners and down streets with names that still ring like angelus bells inside my head—Cottage Grove; Vernon; Rhodes; Vincennes, where I was born; Calumet, where the family lives most vividly still in my dream life and in my heart's recollection. All of these blocks are now radically altered, our centers of communal life now vanished, our vibrant street life sadly diminished. Once bright windows are barred, our nurturing neighbor systems scattered.

The families we knew have long since dispersed to Park Manor and Chatham, Kenwood and Hyde Park. Our old neighborhood had been a crazy-quilt of small family houses, six-flat apartment buildings, and the neat brick structures of the Ida B.

Wells homes, that public housing community of low-rise apartments once surrounded by trees and flowers, now a mile-square battlefield of dirt yards and barred windows. There is no longer a neighborly continuum with semipermeable boundaries, a rich medley of working and professional people, musicians and gamblers, writers and door-to-door insurance men; now the boundaries are sharply drawn. The old neighborhood is bifurcated, half given over to high-rise public housing projects with steel-mesh galleries, where mostly single parents struggle with poverty, their unsupervised children playing far below. The other half comprises gleaming skyscrapers, private housing developments for the affluent, whose children also play far below their parents' gaze, but accompanied by paid baby-sitters. And never the twain shall meet.

Day hated to drive through those streets. It angered her that people had allowed what she called "this ruination" to happen. But I am bound ineluctably to these ghostly concourses, to the intimate avenues of my mid-century Near South Side, to numberless June afternoons exactly like this one, a long ago time in Chicago. Passing 47th Street and King Drive, I began to hum, without thinking, "Evening shadows make me blue, when each weary day is through. How I long to be with you, My Happiness." My father had loved that song, and once, when I was ten or eleven years old, he had taken me to the Met Record Shop on 47th to buy an Ella Fitzgerald recording of it so I could practice for a children's talent show at the Regal Theater. When the appointed day came, we all rode the Number 3 South Park bus down to the competition. As far as I know, that was the only time my mother ever entered the doors of that theater. She didn't like what she called vaudeville, but she would go anywhere to cheer her children on. She, my father, and the family had been smugly sure that I would win, and therefore, so was I. All of us sat in stunned silence when it was announced that I hadn't made it to the second round. I remember being profoundly embarrassed, but my father resolved the situation by marching all seven of us out forthwith, en masse, declaring the entire competition unworthy of the family's involvement. We went home and my mother served up black walnut ice cream.

I stopped now to buy a carton of that ice cream, knowing it would make her smile, though she wouldn't eat more than a couple of spoonfuls.

In less than a week our mother would die here in the old neighborhood, here on Prairie Avenue in Mercy Hospital. *Our* hospital was always Michael Reese, but her grandson Skip was a resident physician at Mercy, and his wife, Maryclare, was a nurse there, so we were assured that she was cared for with un-wavering attention and watched over superbly.

My car next found its way across Pershing Road. Passing the corner where Woods Drugstore was, I paused in front of our old high school, named for the great radical abolitionist orator Wen-dell Phillips. In the 1940s and 1950s its principals were legend-ary, the stately, awesome Maudelle Bousfield and, later, the elegant Virginia Lewis, who had a Ph.D. from Harvard. Our mother had attended evening classes at Phillips when she had first come to Chicago, hoping to finish the high school diploma she never acquired. All five of the Rone children had gone there, and several of our photos are ensconced in the Phillips Hall of Fame along the main-floor corridors, which also house football trophies honoring the celebrated Buddy Young, a classmate of our oldest sister, Zoe.

Within these polished halls we had learned what was then called Negro History from one Ms. Virginia Toles, writing book reports on W. E. B. Du Bois and Booker T. Washington and reading aloud the insistent choric rhythms of Robert Hayden's *Middle Passage*. We had bought blue and white notebooks with *PHS* embossed on the cover from Nick and Angel across Prairie Avenue, where we also bought potato chips and hot sauce to be savored on slow walks home from school, swim meets, or dances at the Wabash Y.

Just around a corner or two, I turned past the South Side

Community Art Center, where friends took drawing and painting classes. My brother Arthur was the only visually gifted one of
the Rones, and he went downtown for his classes—he had won
a scholarship to the Art Institute's Junior School. His specialty
was caricature, but his skill at drawing meticulously helped me
to pass biology, since I simply could never visually reconstruct
the human anatomy or even draw a simple diagram of a flower.
In our family we exchanged skills freely. Jay was a whiz at equa-
tions, Audrey could create the most effective group leadership
strategies, and it was common knowledge that I could help you
find any word in the English language you might ever need.

My linguistic talent was usually thought to be a good and
useful contribution to the family skill bank, but its value was
called into question on at least one occasion: my father's cousin
Harper Roberts had once looked at me probingly—I was about
fourteen or fifteen years old at the time—and pronounced that
I would *never* get a husband: "You have too many words in your
mouth is what the problem is." Of course, my father, outraged,
vigorously took issue with that, and my mother retorted by asking Harper if he had ever written one good book report in his
life, or ever read one decent book, for that matter. Any of her
girls could write well enough for the *Chicago Tribune*, she said,
and "Look at this"—she couldn't keep the boys away from our
door. We did revel in the role of tutor to our older brothers and
also, not infrequently, to our boyfriends.

Deep in such recollection, I had a primal urge to drive past the
old Hardin Square Library; instead, I lamented that the lovely
old building had been torn down to make room for the Dan Ryan
Expressway. Whole paragraphs from library books ran through
my mind. In sixth grade, I had gone through the usual Louisa May
Alcott phase, and Day had read *Little Women* along with me because I asked her to, begging her to tell which of the March girls
reminded her of her own. She had said she could see why I
identified with Jo, but she thought I had a lot of Beth in me. Of
course, Audrey, my own baby sister, was something like Amy,
the youngest of the Marches, but then, too, with something of

the take-chargeness of Meg. According to Day, characters in books were never as complicated or as uneven as real people. She understood stereotype without knowing the word.

I drove across 31st Street, where so much of our community life had been centered. Saturday mornings were the time for up-the-street, down-the-street excursions, when we bought dry goods and staples, live chickens and laces, and occasional treats from the OK Candy Store. We sat for family photos at Deloris Studios, and our father went on Saturday mornings to the barber there on the corner of 31st and Indiana, across from the Terrace Theater, where we sat riveted to weekly double features of movies like *Blood and Sand* and *The Corsican Brothers*, and Lowell Thomas's newsreels cheering on American soldiers—"our boys" overseas. We shopped at Gerstein's, *our* grocery store, although we bought coffee at the A&P, where you could grind your own from 8 O'Clock Coffee bags full of dark, fragrant beans. Everywhere, there were *our* own places. Beyond 31st Street, we occasionally took the Cottage Grove streetcar down to 43rd, to Grove Furniture Store, which was *ours*, as opposed to the store owned by L. Fish, whose daughter later was my classmate at the University of Chicago. When someone we knew died, Leak's or Rayner's funeral homes, and not Jackson's or Sims's, were *ours*.

Pondering the ubiquity of this designation of what was *ours*, I have begun to understand that such emphatic investment of meaning in family choice served a positive, if subconscious, psychosocial purpose. Small choices functioned as significant victories of selfhood. If the range and scope of our choices were necessarily constrained by racial discrimination and inimical power structures, then whatever choices we did make had to be clear, decisive, and *volitional*. Within communities of color, oppressive structures have historically been stripped of power by people's quiet insistence on creating strong personal paradigms.

I am reminded of a story told about W. E. B. Du Bois' first journey to the South. Encountering an old black sharecropper who appeared to be worn and exhausted, Du Bois inquired as to how the man could continue to work his life away farming a little corner of land owned by someone else. Looking the great sociologist straight in the eye, the man replied quietly, "Well, Mr. Professor, it's like this. Yes, you could say that this land here belongs to somebody else, and in one way, you'd be right. But the way I look at it, this little piece of God's earth is *my* little plot. I plow it. I plant it. I water it. I harvest it. When it produces, I know that I had a part in it, right along with my Maker. The way I look at it, while surely this farm belongs to somebody else, this right here where we are standing is *my* little plot. That's what matters to me."

In this way, Michael Reese was *our* hospital, but my mother was to die at Mercy, where I now drove slowly into the parking lot. The old, closed-looking red brick façade was augmented by a new glass entrance, but the same wimpled nuns moved serenely through the corridors in groups of two or three, conjuring up my childhood awareness of their inescapable resemblance to penguins. I was the only one of all the Rone children who had been inside the walls at Mercy in the old days. For several years, I had been afflicted by a persistent sinus condition, and Mercy was where my mother had taken me for weekly treatments with a singularly disgusting medication called Dr. Barnes's Argyrol. What I remember is my nice doctor with the Italian name, the crispness of his white hospital jackets, and the strength and tenderness of my mother's hands as she held my head back for the doctor as he injected that awful stuff into my nasal cavities.

Now, on my own, with no one to hold my hand or my head, I walked like an automaton through the doors at Mercy, into the elevator, and down the corridor, to where my mother, a small figure in the snow-white bed, lay dying. As always, as I entered she looked up—"Hello dahr-ling," in the slowed-down Southern way—and smiled deeply as I bent over her for a kiss. As always, I breathed in her familiar combination of delicacy and strength. Her fingers were still amazingly strong, though at each visit I sucked in my breath at the palpable weakening. She smelled of lemons. Moving away from her, I had trouble straightening up, as my back was still stiff from an earlier injury. She noticed, unchangeably vigilant where the well-being of her children was concerned. What she said then was, "Here, dahr-ling—take one of these pillows from behind my head. I don't need both of them, and these hospital chairs are too hard on your back." A few days later she died, but I think it was at that moment that I decided there had to be a book about a mother like that.

EPILOGUE

When we had to plan our mother's funeral in those days just after she died, when we were at our most tribal, we remembered her discomfort with lady preachers and had to say no when Audrey's close friend, the Rev. Sandra Wilson, one of the first black women ordained as an Episcopal priest, offered to lead the service. We just could not have Day Shepherd Rone's funeral conducted by a lady preacher, even, or perhaps especially, a great lady preacher. Sandy did read that Ecclesiastes scripture about time and seasons, though, which Day had known by heart—we thought that would be okay. My own rector, Sam Lloyd, a white Mississippian, offered a beautiful homily, tender and funny and intimate, and not too churchy, his soft Southern sounds somehow hearkening back to Day's beginnings. The service itself was conducted by a wonderful young black seminarian, Jesse Knox, who handled the whole thing exactly right.

We did not have the funeral in a church. Day's funeral was in a burial parlor in the old neighborhood run by a family whose multiple branches were tangled in our family's history. There were a few problems, or "challenges" as people today like to say, that followed on the decision to go with this particular burial parlor. First of all, their theme color was sky-blue. We thought Day would have asked, "Why in the world are we having this *sky-blue* foolishness?" Everybody knew black is the color for funerals, and in spite of the fact that some people have come to ignore that tradition, our family always wears black to funerals. Having signed up with this place, where we were subject to sky-blue funeral cars and all manner of sky-blue appurtenance, we drew the line at sky-blue funeral program cards. We just couldn't have it, and the burial parlor people, not too happy with our recalcitrance, refused to change their practice. So we had to rush around and get programs printed somewhere else. In black and white.

Then the funeral cars prohibited smoking. Now if one *does* smoke (some in our family do and some of us don't), en route to one's mother's funeral is a time when one pretty much *needs* to smoke. My brother was enraged. Day would have been outraged. We had to enter the burial parlor via a side door and be led into the pew, so there was no way for him to smoke. We are Day's willful children, though, so he found a way.

Finally, after a long ride in the hermetic sky-blue funeral limo to the cemetery where most of our extended tribe and nearly the whole black South Side is buried, we were shepherded to our places—The Family—Arthur, our mother's only remaining son, the last Rone patriarch, tall and solemn, secretly yearning for a cigarette; Zoe, sorrowing, veiled, understanding that she must suddenly wear the mantle of clan matriarch; Audrey, our mother's baby, the one who lived most closely with Day in these last years, now unable to imagine anything called Home without our mother in it; me, the literary one, seeing our history passing, one life and an entire way of life; there, too, all of our husbands and wives and children, all of the grandchildren; and the spirits of Day's absent men, our father who preceded her in death by twenty-one years, and her firstborn son Jay, gone nearly twenty years too, his passing never actually real to us, permanently impossible to absorb.

Here we all were, confirming and affirming that which binds us. There is so much beauty among us, so much the work of our mother's hands. Some of us were weeping, some praying quietly. And then, just as the burial parlor workers began to lower the coffin into the grave, the borders of which were draped in sky-blue, the coffin tilted sharply and would not slip smoothly into the ground. There was a very brief interim before they could finally manipulate the chains and ropes and deliver the body into the space that had been prepared for it. In that brief passing moment between this world and the next, the family smiled at one another. A nonvolitional but incontrovertible look passed among all of us, shared like a Holy Communion chalice. The rhythm of the family is so finely tuned that we were shaking our heads in unison, looking up to heaven because we could all hear that same clear voice: it was our mother, shaking her head and saying, "Can't these trifling people with all this sky-blue foolishness get anything right?" Amen, Mother. Amen.

In time we put the gravestone in, with the basic facts engraved just right, the way she wanted them: *Thelma Shepherd Rone, Mother, July 20, 1899–June 10, 1986*. Audrey and Tony planted a pink azalea on our mother's grave, which, in subsequent years, flowered profusely, as though nourished by some subterranean stream. Ultimately the cemetery people had to ask our permission to uproot the whole thing because it was growing too wildly and covering up other people's gravestones. The grandchildren speak once in a while of breaking the rules and planting another one. For now we just take her cut flowers or an occasional small potted plant. Day did so love all things that grow. She loved their variegated shapes and colors and fragrances, their transformation from seed to unanticipatable bloom. She understood the investment of daily care; that had its place. But her delight, always, was in the amazement of the flower.

ACKNOWLEDGMENTS

This book of our mother's stories owes everything to our clan, those without whom the recollections would never have lived this long. First, to those who have left this planet but are critical in our memory: Most of all to our mother, Thelma Shepherd Rone, just plain Day to those who loved her, whose spirit continues to enlighten all our generations. Then to our father, John Drayton Rone, the other half of the remarkable pair who shaped us so skillfully and with such clarity. The longer memories were kept alive through the years by their first daughter, Zoe, and by their first son, Jay. They both died too soon, but they are a part of the bedrock of who we are. Then to the living, to Arthur Shepherd Rone and to Audrey Rone Peeples, my beloved brother and sister who remain to laugh with me the way our mother did; to call me to task; to add to, to critique, to live within these stories; to illuminate and give meaning to a way of living in and *with* family. To their spouses, John Patterson, Melvin Lucille Rone, the late Lena Waller Rone, and especially Anthony Peeples, so deeply missed, who so believed that this book had to be written, and who gratefully lived long enough to read the first draft of the manuscript.

We perceive the inherited gifts of family wisdom still unfolding as we rear our children and our grandchildren, those newer members of our clan. To John Drayton Rone III, Dr. John E. Patterson Jr., Dr. Drayton Rone Patterson (Butchie, Skip, and Scooter), Dr. Arthur Rone Jr., David and Christopher Rone, Jennifer and Michael Peeples, and all of their spouses and progeny. To my daughters, Claire Hartfield Harris, Lisa Hartfield Davé, Karen Hartfield Benedict, and Lynn Hartfield Thoman, the fabulous four, who have endowed the family with such gifts of dignity and grace, and whose husbands, Philip Harris, Peter Davé, Hubbard Benedict, and Eric Thoman, have added their own strengths to the family. To our eight gifted grandchildren, Emily, Caroline, and Corinne Harris; Zena and Nathan Davé; Maxwell and Graham Benedict, and Elena Isabelle Thoman. Our mother did not live to know you, but some of you have her eyes, others her spirit. I hope some of you will have her clarity. And finally to my husband Bob Hartfield, who has listened to these stories since he made me his child bride nearly half a century ago, in part because, like all people of sense and sensibility, he loved my mother instantly, knowing a good thing when he saw it.

I would also like to acknowledge others to whom this book owes its life. To the Rockefeller Foundation, whose support allowed me the privilege of writing for many weeks at one of the world's most splendid sites, the Villa Serbelloni on the shores of Lake Como. To the Illinois Humanities Council and to others whose anonymous support was critical in the early months, when disparate notes began to take form as a narrative. To the Aspen Institute, with gratitude for fellowships where I learned the importance of reflecting upon individual experience in wider social and historical contexts. To the Harvard University Center for the Study of World Religions for the special resources afforded me by a valued senior research fellowship.

To a long list of dearly valued friends who have encouraged me all along: Lynne Atherton, Carol Becker, Diana Beliard, Sonya Brock, Greg Cameron, Susanna Coffey, Quinn Delaney, Toni Dewey, Alison Edwards, Barbara Elleman, Julie Ellis, Carol Gaebler, Edith Gaines, Shirley Genther, Roger Gilmore, Jonathan Green, Nancy Greenebaum, Meffie Hastings, Arlene Hirsch, Fredda and Sidney Hyman, Delores Irvin, Jetta Jones,

Mark Krisco, Sara Lawrence-Lightfoot, Dorothy Mandel, Jim and Pamela Morton, Nancy and Stuart Murphy, Vreni Naess, Barbara Pace, Lorenzo Pace, Tony Phillips, Judith Raphael, Catharine Reeve, Anne Roosevelt, Eunita Rushing, Sara Schastok, Lelia Schoenberg, Wini Scott, Diane Seidler, Diann DeWeese Smith, Porter Stewart, Carol Sykes, Audrey Tuggle, Barbara Tzur, Eileen and Ed Wasserman, and Jessie Woods. I offer special gratitude for the life of Gail Westgate, whose deep and caring friendship with me and my family was profoundly important to all of us, and, of course, to the writing of our stories. To Amina Dickerson, Sandra Furey-Gaither, and Isobel Neal, my soul-saving travel gang, who always believed in this book. To Samuel Akainyah, Arnold Aprill, Liz Crowe, Maxine Duster, Nancy Gilpin, Cil Rockwell, Marjory Slavin, Joan Small, Mara Tapp, Maxine and Dan Tropp, and Ragdale Foundation colleagues Alice Ryerson Hayes, Katharine Ravenel, and Susan Tillett: your unwavering insistence that this very personal book was worthwhile for many audiences gave me courage.

To my teachers at Wendell Phillips High School, whose care and mentoring was critical to my early self-definition, especially Mildred Proctor Poreé, and to my teachers and colleagues at the University of Chicago, who honed my thinking and enlarged my vision, especially Charles G. Bell, Bernard O. Brown, Anne Carr, Langdon Gilkey, Clark Gilpin, Charles H. Long, Martin Marty, Paul Ricoeur, Herman Sinaiko, and Anthony Yu. To deep soul poet friends Sterling Plumpp and the late Walter Bradford, who taught me to listen for the personal voice in speech.

To our extended clan: the Shepherd cousins, Connie Shepherd McClendon and Ben, John, and the late Sam Shepherd; the Lehmann cousins, Arlene Sykes Alexander, Bill and Ed Sykes, Rita Lehmann Henry, Clara Lehmann Jackson, and their late sister Kay Lehmann Wilson; Nettie Lehmann Ransom, Irene Ransom Lee, and Benny and Leroy Ransom. Thanks also to Dr. Ann Feldman and Julia Kramer, whose critical genealogical research added dimension to the early stories, and to Nicole Cipriani, whose intelligent and persistent deciphering of reams of raw copy was invaluable in the production of this manuscript. Special gratitude goes to my editor, Robert Devens, whose probing questions and thoughtful suggestions contributed immeasurably to this text, and to Meg Cox for meticulous and responsive copy editing. Finally, profound thanks to my agent, Leslie Breed, and to Paula Barker Duffy, director of the University of Chicago Press, for taking the risk to publish *Another Way Home*.